The Intelligent Consumer:

HOW NOT TO BE A "CONNED-SUMER"

Gershon J. Wheeler

The Intelligent Consumer:
HOW NOT TO BE A "CONNED-SUMER"

RESTON PUBLISHING COMPANY, INC.
A Prentice-Hall Company
RESTON, VIRGINIA 22090

Library of Congress Cataloging in Publication Data

Wheeler, Gershon J
  The intelligent consumer.
  vii, 176 p.
  1. Finance, Personal. 2. Consumer education.
I. Title.
HG179.W52   640.73   74–34209
ISBN 0–87909–364–1

© 1975 by Reston Publishing Company, Inc.
A Prentice-Hall Company
Reston, Virginia 22090

10 9 8 7 6 5 4 3 2

Printed in the United States of America

Table of Contents

Chapter One: *IT'S YOUR MONEY, 1*

Chapter Two: *LIFE INSURANCE, 4*
Premiums, 4   Types of Policies, 7   Forced Savings, 14
What Insurance Should you Buy, 15   Beneficiary, 17
Provisions and Features, 19   Mail Order Insurance, 20
Social Security, 21

Chapter Three: *SAVINGS ACCOUNTS, 24*
Types of "Banks", 26   Safety, 27   Availability, 30
Interest, 31   How to Get More Interest, 36
Convenience, 38   Free Services, 39   Which Institution? 39

Chapter Four: *CHECKING ACCOUNTS & CHARGE
ACCOUNTS, 40*
Checking Accounts, 40   Negotiable Order of
Withdrawal, 42   Charge Accounts, 43   Truth in
Lending, 47

Chapter Five: *AUTOMOTIVE, 49*
Depreciation, 49   Maintenance, 51   Insurance, 52
Finance Charges, 54   New or Used, 55   Upkeep, 57
Tires, 58   Dealing with Dealers, 60   That Second
Car, 63   Optional Equipment, 64

Chapter Six: **SHELTER, 66**
Renting an Apartment, 68   Renting a House, 69
Cost Comparison, 72   Buying a Home, 75   Insurance, 82
Condominiums, 83   Mobile Homes, 88   Your Home
as an Investment, 90

Chapter Seven: **APPLIANCES, 93**
Automatic Washers, 98   Dryers, 102   Refrigerators and
Freezers, 105   Ranges, 113   Dishwashers, 120   Garbage
Disposers, 125   Vacuum Cleaners, 127   Small Kitchen
Appliances, 130   Television Sets, 131

Chapter Eight: **ESTATES, 133**
Community Property, 134   Rules of Intestate
Succession, 134   Wills, 136   Provisions in Your Will, 139
Title by Operation of Law, 140   Probate Proceedings, 142
Estate Planning, 145   Joint Tenancy, 147   Gifts, 148
Testamentary Trusts, 150   Living Trusts, 153   Life
Insurance, 154

Chapter Nine: **RECORD KEEPING, 157**

Chapter Ten: **THEFT AND FRAUD, 164**
Protecting Your Home Against Theft, 164   Protecting
Your Car Against Theft, 166   Frauds, 167   Home
Improvements, 168   Debt Consolidation, 169   Chain
Referral, 169   Fake Contests, 170   Missing Heirs, 170
Unordered Merchandise, 171   Charity Rackets, 171
Business Opportunities, 172   Mail Order, 173   Frauds
Against the Elderly, 175

Preface

The Establishment and its salesmen are conning the American public at virtually every level in the use of food, goods, and energy. You, the consumer, are led to believe that the only way to the Great American Dream is the Establishment's way. You work diligently and spend and save in a conventional manner so that you can own a conventional home with a conventional mortgage. If you have misgivings, you console yourself with the thought that everyone else is doing the same thing.

But perhaps the American dream should not be your dream. The purpose of this book is to show you how to be an intelligent consumer rather than a conventional, even gullible one—how to decide what parts of the American dream are right for you. It explains how you can spend and save intelligently and keep from being *conned* into consuming what you do not need or want.

GERSHON J. WHEELER

Chapter One

It's Your Money

Everyone is after YOUR money. You are constantly bombarded with advertisements urging you to buy every conceivable product and service; and you do respond to these advertisements, even though you are well aware that claims may be exaggerated or even false. As progress brings new products and better construction of older products, advertising is necessary to make the public aware of these developments, and also to create the urge to buy.

Advertisements are not subtle. They promise power, sex, recognition, and self-confidence. You know they stretch the truth, and you are slow to bite, but the effects are cumulative. Thus, after listening to advertisements for more than 50 years extolling the benefits of owning a new car, the public has come to equate the auto with status. The paradox here is that the automobile industry on the one hand is boasting about the improvements that allow you to drive a car for 50,000 trouble-free miles, and on the other hand they urge you to buy a new car every year to keep up with the latest changes in style.

In general, the public is skeptical of all advertising claims, but can be convinced by constant repetition and appeal to basic needs. Some typical examples are found in toothpaste advertisements. A real breakthrough occurred when scientists discovered that stannous fluoride helped prevent cavities in teeth. Procter & Gamble used this ingredient in Crest toothpaste, and advertised that Crest helped prevent tooth decay. This time the advertisement was true, but the public didn't believe it. It was dismissed as another exaggerated claim. An improved advertising campaign has made Crest a best seller, but it is not clear whether this is due to stannous fluoride or to the better advertisements.

Another toothpaste was invented by an advertising man. In effect, the advertiser said, "If we had a striped toothpaste, I could sell it." A method of putting stripes in toothpaste was invented and the toothpaste was put on the market. Although it had no special properties to clean teeth better than other toothpastes, it sold well because of an outstanding advertising campaign.

When a toothpaste is advertised as one that gives the user sex appeal, its attraction is the need for sexual recognition. If a person lacks sex appeal or just thinks he does, he is ready to try anything that promises to furnish this mystic element. The toothpaste may or may not be a good cleaning agent, but as long as it does no harm to the teeth and gums, it may do some good for the user's ego. This particular kind of advertising campaign is quite successful.

Advertisements convince you to buy things you don't need and to spend more than you can afford. Over the years, advertisements have created what might be called a conventional outlook on living. The automobile *is* a status symbol because the advertisements have been saying this for so long that the public now believes it. Thus if nothing else, advertisements induce you to part with your money in a conventional manner, living a conventional life, as the establishment dictates. This is not the way to get the most for your money!

You don't have to be non-conformist to get more for your money; you just have to learn to think as a non-conformist when it comes to money matters. There is no reason why you shouldn't buy something you want, but make sure that *you* really want it and are not buying it because you are told that you ought to want it. A large luxury car is more prestigious and more comfortable than one of the standard models. If you will be using your automobile for long trips, your need for comfort may justify your owning a luxury car. However, "prestige" is largely a product of the advertisers and should not induce you to buy such a car for driving to and from work or for shopping. Don't limit your buying to bare necessities. You want a comfortable home, not one that is barely functional. You may *want* to travel or indulge in expensive hobbies. Do so, not because it's the thing to do, but because that's what you really want.

In spite of the establishment, there is a growing awareness of Consumerism. The Federal government issues many pamphlets and fact sheets explaining how to get more for your money in almost every type of purchase. These are available from the Government Printing Office in Washington, D.C. In addition, there are many consumer groups that furnish advice on particular products. Even manufacturers are getting into the act with booklets explaining what to look for when buying the products they make. Even though these last are obviously biased, they do provide worthwhile information.

It is impossible to cover every aspect of buying in a book such as this. Food or medicine alone could fill a complete book. Instead, some of the larger and more expensive purchases you might make are discussed here, with some recommendations. The most important recommendation is: THINK. Just keep in mind that it's *your* money, and you should be able to spend it as you see fit. If you allow the establishment to dictate how and what you buy, you are not spending it wisely or even as you would want to if you thought about it. Think, and get more for your money.

Chapter Two

Life Insurance

Millions of dollars are wasted each year in overpayments for life insurance. Most people have the wrong kind of coverage and are spending too much for the coverage they have. Unfortunately, most life insurance salesmen are interested in selling the policies on which they get the highest commissions rather than those that are best for the purchasers. Life insurance companies also have a profit motive for selling high-cost policies. Therefore, you should be wary of advice offered through literature published by insurance companies and advice proffered by their agents. The primary purpose of life insurance is to provide financial assistance when the breadwinner dies. If you keep this in mind when buying insurance, you can save thousands of dollars in premiums during your lifetime.

PREMIUMS

The amount of money you pay for your insurance is called the *premium* and it is based on your life expectancy. Your life expectancy in turn is based upon your age, sex, and to some extent upon your occupation. When you purchase insurance, you and the company sign a contract that obligates the company to pay your beneficiary the face value of the policy when you die, if your insurance is still in force. You can cancel this contract at any time by simply not paying the premium when it is due, but the company cannot break the contract as long as you continue paying your premiums. Note that if you withhold pertinent information, about your health for example, the company can cancel the policy during the first two years, but at the end of the two-year period, the policy is incontestable. However, if at any time even after the two year period is up, the company learns that you lied about your age, the company will use your correct age in calculating benefits. For example, when you first buy a $10,000 policy you state your age as 32, even though you are 35. The premium for age 32 for your policy is $170, and you pay this amount every year. When you die, the company learns that your true age at the start of the policy was 35 and you should have been paying $200 for $10,000 worth of insurance. The $170 you actually paid entitled you to 170/200 of $10,000 worth of insurance or $8500, and this is the amount your beneficiary will get.

Although all insurance companies use the same table for life expectancy, their insurance premiums differ widely. The premium rate is supposed to be based on the average number of expected deaths. To this the companies add an amount to pay their expenses and leave a reasonable profit. In any one year, however, the number of deaths may exceed the expected average; to take care of this contingency, companies charge more than they should. If these excess funds are not used during the year, the companies pay back the difference to the policy holders. The payment is called a *dividend*, but it is really a reduction in the premium and is not taxable as income. The true premium is the difference between what is paid and the dividend returned.

When dividends are paid or expected to be paid on a policy, the policy is called *participating*. The premium rate is fixed in a participating policy, but the dividend rate is not. In fact, even though the policy is of the participating type, the company is under no obligation to pay a dividend, and conceivably would omit the dividend if too many policy holders died during a given year. In practice, they charge enough to take care of all possible extra expenses, so that some dividend is always paid. In effect, although the premium rate is specified in the policy, the company is able to manipulate the true premiums by varying the amount of its dividends.

Non-participating policies do not receive dividends. Premiums are usually lower than the stated premiums in participating policies because no dividend will be paid. Companies that issue non-participating policies presumably have calculated their expenses carefully and charge the policy holder a premium close to the theoretical minimum.

In practice, these companies also fear unexpected expenses and thus raise the premiums to cover anything that might arise. It is not really possible to state categorically that one type is cheaper than the other. When buying insurance, you should look at past dividend records of companies issuing participating policies and compare the net costs with the premiums of non-participating policies.

If you have a participating policy, the dividend is always paid on the policy anniversary, and you have a few options as to how you receive it:

1. You can take the cash. You might do this if you don't plan to renew your policy.

2. You can apply the dividend as a reduction of your next premium. This is the most common practice.

3. You can buy additional *paid-up* insurance with the dividend. *Paid-up* means that the insurance you buy is completely paid for and you need make no further payments for it. The paid-up insurance stays in force for the rest of your life.

4. You can buy one-year term insurance without a physical examination.

5. You can leave the money with the insurance company as in a savings account. The company does pay interest, but generally at a lower rate than you could get elsewhere.

Premiums may be paid annually, semiannually, quarterly, or monthly. Annually is the cheapest. Insurance companies add an interest charge if you prefer to pay in installments. The true interest is much more than it seems at first glance. As a simple example suppose that your annual premium is $206. If you pay semiannually you are told it will cost only 3% more or $212, in two payments of $106 each. This seems like a low rate, but is it? When you make the first payment of $106 instead of $206, you are in effect borrowing $100. At the end of six months you pay another $106. So you have paid $6 interest to borrow $100 for six months. Thus the rate is 12% per year. The true rate for quarterly installments is higher, and for monthly installments it may be more than 25% per year.

Note that insurance premiums do not come under the Truth in Lending Act. The reason is that you can cancel your policy between installments since you have no contract forcing you to continue making payments. Each installment is considered a separate contractual obligation on the company to insure you for a specific time rather than an installment on a longer term contract.

TYPES OF POLICIES

There are two general types of policies. One is pure insurance. You pay a premium. When you die your beneficiary collects. If you cancel the policy before you die, you get nothing back. The other type combines straight insurance with what insurance companies would have you believe is a savings account. There are many variations. *Whole Life* is insurance that you pay for during your lifetime. It is also called *ordinary life, straight life, living insurance,* or *permanent insurance.* The premium is higher than for pure life insurance because the whole life policy has a cash value which you can collect whenever you cancel the policy. This is presumably an attraction, but it is not really a savings account. A realistic evaluation of insurance policies that include a so-called savings feature, begins on page 10.

Limited payment life insurance policies require that you make payments for a specified time, such as 20 years, and then you are insured for life. These policies also have a savings feature and are simply more expensive variations of ordinary life.

Endowment policies are the most expensive. These combine insurance plus a savings account, but you can't get both. If you die during the life of the policy, your beneficiary receives only the sum stipulated as the face value of the policy. If you outlive the policy, *you* collect the face value, *but you are no longer insured.* Typical endowment plans are 20-year endowments and endowment at age 65.

Term insurance is pure insurance in its simplest form. When you buy term insurance, the company agrees to pay your beneficiary the face value of the policy, if you die within the time specified (the term). At the end of the term, your insurance terminates. You can renew it by buying a new policy. Most insurance companies offer *renewable term* insurance. That is, you can buy a new term policy at the expiration of the old one without a physical examination. When you buy an insurance policy, you generally, are required to pass a physical examination. Insurance companies are understandably reluctant to insure a person with a short life expectancy. The *renewable* feature of renewable term is only the waiving of this physical examination. Each time you buy a new term policy whether you renew your old one or start afresh, you pay a higher rate than you did on the old one since you are older. The older you are, the more likely you are to die before the expiration of the policy, and therefore the higher the rate.

When you buy term insurance, you are in effect betting the insurance company that you will die before the expiration of the term. The company is betting you will live. This is a bet you are perfectly willing to lose; but if you should die, the proceeds of the policy will provide needed financial assistance for your beneficiary. If you do live and thus lose the bet, the money spent for the insurance was spent needlessly, but how could you tell? To prevent a financial catastrophe for your beneficiary you need insurance; but since there is always the possibility that you may outlive the policy, it is important to get the best insurance for your needs at a cost within your means.

Term insurance is available for 5 years, 10 years, and 20 years. For special situations, special term policies are available. For example, the air travel insurance you buy at an airport just before a flight is term insurance for the duration of the flight. Another special type of term insurance is the decreasing term policy which is usually bought to pay off a mortgage in the event of death of the homeowner. The term is the length of the mortgage, and the face value of the policy decreases as the mortgage decreases.

In general, the longer the term, the more the insurance company will charge for the insurance. Typically, a $1000 5-year term policy at age 30 may cost $8.50 per year, as against $9.25 for a 10-year term. However, the 5-year term must be renewed at age 35, and at that age the rate might be $10.00 for another 5-year term. If you live the whole 10 years, 5-year term policies would cost you 5 × $8.50 plus 5 × $10 or $92.50, and the 10-year term policy at $9.25 annually would also cost you $92.50, so there seems to be no difference. However, if you died before the ten years were up, you would have saved money by buying the 5-year term and renewing it. The situation is also affected somewhat by dividends that the company pays; but in general, you do better by buying the shortest term policy available (one year, if possible) and renewing it when it expires.

Insurance companies do not let you renew term policies indefinitely, since as you grow older the chances increase that you will die before the expiration of the term. Most companies put an age limit of 65 on term policies, but a few permit renewals up to age 70.

Term policies are usually *convertible*. This means that you can convert the term insurance to ordinary life or any other type of insurance (except term) at any policy anniversary. You usually have two options as to the premium you will pay for the new policy. If you convert the term as of the current date, your new policy is dated as of the time of conversion, and you pay the rate for that policy for whatever your age is at that time. Alternatively you can back date the policy to any earlier date and pay the rate for your age at that date, but in this case you have to make up the difference in premiums between the rate of the new policy and what you actually paid from the indicated date of conversion to the present.

Note that if you stop paying premiums on your insurance, the policy is cancelled. If you have term insurance, at any policy anniversary you can drop part of it and continue paying for the rest. The same option is open to you when you renew or when you convert. Thus, if you have $50,000 worth of term insurance, you can renew $40,000 and drop $10,000, whenever you feel you need less insurance. Similarly, at age 65 you might decide to convert only part of your term insurance since at that age your children are no longer dependent and you need less insurance.

The two options for conversion (as of the current date or back-dated) both sound expensive. If you convert at the current date, you pay a much higher premium. If you backdate, your premium is lower, (although still higher than that for the term insurance), but you are required to pay a large lump sum to the insurance company. Actually, the added expense can be minimized in both cases, because you need less insurance. In fact, if you combine a good savings program with term insurance when you first buy your policy, you should not need any insurance after age 65. See Table 3 on page 13.

If you decide to convert as of the current date, your premium is much larger. For example, at the last renewal of your 5-year term policy, your $50,000 of insurance might have a premium of $1500.

This is reduced by whatever dividends the company pays. At age 65, the same amount of ordinary insurance might cost $3200 a year, more than double the term premium. If you want to convert the whole amount and still avoid too great a financial burden, you could borrow about $1200 a year using your policy as security, for the loan. You may be able to borrow from the insurance company. Now your net cost is only $2000, plus the interest on the loan. When you die, the loan is paid off, and your beneficiary gets the balance of the $50,000.

If you decide to convert by backdating, your premium may even be less than the latest term premium but there is a lump sum payment to be made, However, the new policy will have a *cash and loan* value which is the same as it would be if you had actually bought that policy on the backdate. You use this loan value to pay the difference, so that you have no out-of-pocket expense. Again, when you die, your beneficiary receives the face value of the policy less the amount borrowed.

Whole Life Insurance salesmen like to stress the *savings* feature of whole life policies. The premium for whole life is much higher than that for term insurance, but the whole life policy has a *cash value*. That is, if you *cancel* the insurance you can get back the cash value stated in the policy. Also, if you are strapped for cash at anytime, you can borrow an amount up to the cash value at a comparably low rate of interest. If you should die while the loan is outstanding, the loan is repaid from the proceeds of the policy, and your beneficiary gets the difference.

During the first year or two, a whole life policy has no cash value since the company's cost of administration and commissions use up most of the premium. After that the company in effect uses part of the premium to furnish you pure term insurance and puts the balance into the cash value of the policy. The cash in your "savings account" draws interest but only at 2% or 3%. However, the cash value does grow, and if you live a reasonable length of time, you could cancel your policy and get back almost all you spent in premiums. Your insurance salesman's pitch runs something like this: If you buy term insurance, at the end of 20 years you will have paid $3000 and at that time (if you live) you will have nothing. On the other hand, if you buy whole life, you will have paid $7000 in 20 years, but at that time the cash value would be about $6500. You can cancel the policy and get back this $6500 so that your net cost for 20 years is only $500 instead of $3000. Furthermore, as the cash value of the policy was building up, it was money that you could borrow in case of financial emergency.

The arguments in the preceding paragraph may sound convincing, but the salesman has deliberately omitted a few important facts. The savings feature is largely illusory. If you keep the policy until you die, your beneficiary gets only the face value and the savings disappear. Furthermore, if the cash value is savings, why should you have to pay interest to borrow it? It should be obvious that you can do better buying term insurance and putting the extra money in a savings account. The arithmetic is simple. The following table gives some typical rates for $10,000 of term insurance and for whole life. These may vary from one company to the next, but are representative.

Assume you want to buy a $50,000 life insurance policy at age 25. If you buy whole life, it will cost you $675 a year, every year as long as you keep the policy. If you buy term insurance for the same amount it will cost $250 each year for the first 5 years, then $270 for the next, $300 a year for the third 5-year period, and $365 a year for the fourth, assuming you renew the policy each time it expires. If you are willing to allocate $675 a year to buy the insurance, as you would have to do if you bought whole life, you can buy term insurance and put the difference in premiums in a savings account. Thus, for the first 5 years you would pay $250 for insurance and bank $425 each year. The money in your savings account grows by compound interest. During the second 5-year interval you will bank $405 per year. During the third it is down to $375 a year and then $310 per year for the fourth. The next table indicates how your savings account would have

TABLE 1 RATES FOR $10,000 OF INSURANCE

Age	25	30	35	40	45	50	55	60
5-Year Term (Renewable)	$ 50	54	60	73	105	150	210	300
Whole Life Policy	$135	160	188	225	275	335	420	510

TABLE 2 GROWTH OF SAVINGS ACCOUNT

Age	Total Premiums Paid	Total Deposited in Savings	Amount in Savings Account
30	1,250	2,125	2,430
35	2,600	4,150	5,415
40	4,100	6,025	9,053
45	5,925	7,575	13,323

---

grown at a modest rate of 5% compounded annually. You in fact get higher rates, compounded daily.

Note that even after 5 years, the $2125 you have deposited has grown to $2430. At age 45, 20 years after you started, you have deposited $7575, but interest has increased your account to $13,323. How about cash value? That cash in your savings account is *your* cash. If you want to use it for an emergency, you don't have to pay interest for the privilege. Notice that it is actually higher than the amount you paid in premiums, which is not true of the cash value of a whole life policy. Also, this savings account doesn't disappear when you die. If you die at age 45, your beneficiary receives the $50,000 from your life insurance *plus* the $13,323 in your savings account.

If you look at Table 1 again, you will notice that if you renew your policy at age 45, you have only a slight savings in premiums over what you would have if you bought a whole life policy at age 25. At 50 and later, the term costs more than the whole life at 25, so that it seems that if you continued to live, there would be no savings in term by the time you got to age 65. However, if you start out with the idea that you want $50,000 of funds available for your beneficiary, you can see that as your savings account grows, representing cash available, you need less insurance to make the total funds $50,000. In Table 2, you will notice that at the end of the first 5-year period, you have $2430. Thus you need only $47,570 of insurance to make $50,000 available for your beneficiary. Rounding this to the nearest $1,000, you renew $48,000 of your term insurance and drop $2000. Using this method of renewing at each 5-year interval only the amount of term insurance needed to make the total funds at least $50,000, your savings account builds up faster, as shown in Table 3. A $50,000 whole life policy costs $675 a year if taken out at age 25, and this amount is used as the basis of savings.

When you buy your first term policy at age 25, you need $50,000. Since the cost is $5 per $1000, your premium is thus $250. This is $425 less than the $675 needed to buy the same amount of whole life insurance, so you put $425 in a savings account. After doing this every year for five years, your savings account has accumulated $2430. This is shown in the first line of Table 3. Now you renew $48,000 to keep the total funds available above $50,000. At age 30, term insurance costs $5.40 per $1000, so your premium for the $48,000 is $259.20. This is $415.80 less than the $675 whole life premium so you bank $415.80 each year for five years. Your savings account is now $5477. For the next five year period you need only $45,000 of insurance. If you continue as shown, at age 65 your savings account has $44,999 in it. At this point you don't need insurance. The $44,999 in the bank plus social security benefits are more than enough to cover your insurance needs.

If you had started your savings program and term insurance purchases at age 40 instead of age 25, at age 65 you still would have accumulated a savings account nearly equal to your insurance coverage. Referring to Table 1, you see that whole life insurance at age 40 costs $22.50 per $1000 rather than the $13.50 cost at age 25. Term at age 40 costs $7.30 per $1000. The difference is $15.20. Thus for a

TABLE 3 SAVINGS GROWTH, MAINTAINING $50,000 AVAILABLE FUNDS

Age Period	Premium per $1000 per Year	Insurance Needed	Savings Added per Year	Total Savings at End of Period
25–30	$ 5.00	$50,000	$425.00	$ 2,430
30–35	5.40	48,000	415.80	5,477
35–40	6.00	45,000	405.00	9,304
40–45	7.30	41,000	375.30	14,017
45–50	10.50	36,000	297.00	19,583
50–55	15.00	31,000	210.00	26,188
55–60	21.00	24,000	171.00	34,393
60–65	30.00	16,000	195.00	44,999

$50,000 policy, you would bank $760 per year for the first five years. Your savings account grows much faster and again at age 65 you have no further need for insurance.

Tables 1, 2, and 3 are based on 5-year renewable term policies, which are readily available. Some companies issue one-year renewable term, and if you buy this and follow the general procedures illustrated in Table 3, you will build up an even larger savings account. This happens because you can reduce your insurance at more frequent intervals as your savings account reaches the next $1000 level, instead of waiting the full 5-year period. However, if your insurance company allows you to drop part of your term insurance between 5-year anniversaries you can do almost as well with the 5-year term as with one-year term.

Other types   Everything covered in the preceding section on whole life insurance applies also to limited payment insurance and to endowment policies, only more so. Premiums are higher than for whole life. If you buy term insurance and bank the difference in premiums, you will have just as much coverage at less net cost.

FORCED SAVINGS

Your insurance salesman will tell you that most people cannot discipline themselves to bank the difference in premiums regularly, and even if they do, the temptation to use the extra money in the savings account to buy a car or T.V. or take a trip is too strong. This may be true, but you should still realize that the savings feature of cash value insurance is a mirage. When you die, all the extra savings disappear, and your beneficiary gets only the specified face value of the policy.

One way to resist the temptation to withdraw your savings is to open a separate savings account specifically for insurance. This account should be a joint account with your beneficiary. Some precaution must be taken to make sure that neither of you are tempted to withdraw funds, and the simplest is to require both signatures on a withdrawal request. Each year you pay into the account the full premium that you would have to pay for a whole life policy. You authorize your insurance company to withdraw enough to pay for your term insurance each year. As far as you are concerned the savings account is your insurance company. Each year you pay into it what you would have to pay for whole life, and each year the savings account pays your real insurance company the term premium. Every 5 years, you drop some of your term insurance as shown in Table 3, but you continue making the same annual payments. Your savings account will grow as indicated in Table 3.

If you have better willpower, you can deposit only the difference in your savings account, and pay the insurance company directly. Even if you have excellent discipline, it is a good idea to maintain a separate savings account for your insurance *cash value* and to feel that the funds in it will not be touched until age 65.

WHAT INSURANCE SHOULD YOU BUY?

If you have read the preceding sections you know that term insurance is preferable to any other type, and that you can get the effect of other types of insurance by combining term insurance with a savings account. Term insurance is indeed cheaper than other types and the pay-off is the same in case of death. The so-called savings features of other policies vanish when you die.

Does this mean you should rush out and buy a lot of term insurance? Not necessarily. Before you buy any insurance there are many other questions to ask and answer. Do you really need insurance? Who in your family should be insured? When should you buy insurance? How much? Then finally, what type best suits your needs?

The answers to these questions are obvious, if you keep in mind the basic reason for buying life insurance. If the family income ceases when the breadwinner dies, life insurance can provide the necessary financial assistance. This is the purpose for buying insurance. If your family is dependent on *your* salary and if that salary stops when you die, then *you* should have insurance to provide an income after you are gone.

Do you need insurance? If you have no dependents, you do not need insurance. Insurance salesmen have many arguments to convince you to buy insurance right now, whether you need it or not. For example, premiums are lower, or you may not be able to pass the required physical examination later when you need insurance. But, pay attention to the reason for buying insurance and if you don't need it, don't buy it. If your spouse works or has an independent income, you don't need insurance. If your income is from royalties which will continue long after your death, you don't need insurance.

Should you insure your children? Many agents try to sell an endowment policy for young children to provide a fund to pay college expenses when they reach 18. This is a case of misplaced emphasis. If you should die in the interim, who will pay the premiums on such a policy for your child? It is more important to insure *your* life, so that if you die, money is available for your child's college education. At the same time, you should start to build up a savings account to provide the needed funds for the college education. You will find that term insurance on your own life plus deposits in the savings account cost less than premiums for an endowment policy on your child.

By the same reasoning, a wife should not be insured unless she is also a breadwinner and loss of her income would create a problem. When both husband and wife work and there are no children there is probably no need for either to have life insurance. If there are dependent children, then both should be insured.

When you have dependents, how much insurance do you need? It might be nice to leave your dependents financially independent for life, but the amount of insurance needed would be prohibitively expensive and besides it is not necessary. You should figure on providing your widow with enough money to live on, including an allowance for bringing up the children, plus enough to provide a good college education for each child. Widows with dependent children also receive social security benefits. This is also part of your insurance program and is discussed more fully later in this chapter. Thus, your insurance needs change. When you first marry, if your wife does not work, you need enough to provide an income for her. Realistically, you are just starting out and probably cannot afford the amount of insurance needed to guarantee your salary to her for the rest of her life. In truth, you don't need much, since your wife is young enough to learn a skill and get a job or to remarry. As you both get older, whether or not you have children, you will probably want to increase your insurance. If you have children, you will definitely want to increase your insurance. When the children have left home and are on their own, you can decrease your insurance again. After age 65, when social security income augments your insurance, you can drop most of your policies. If you have maintained a savings program over the years, your insurance needs decrease as your savings grow.

There is no doubt that with term insurance you get the most for the money. Buy the shortest renewable term available. Usually this will mean a 5-year term, but inquire about one-year renewable term. It is important that the insurance be *renewable*. From a practical standpoint, if you have young children, you should buy as much term insurance as you can afford. But don't neglect your savings program. It is not necessary to keep decreasing your term insurance, as your savings grow. The purpose of the examples in Table 3 is to show that term insurance in conjunction with a savings account is better than other forms of insurance. You probably cannot afford to buy as much as you would like when your children are very young, so you buy what you can afford and do not decrease it as your savings account grows. In fact, as your income increases, you might increase both your insurance and your savings account until your insurance is at a satisfactory level.

BENEFICIARY

The *beneficiary* of your insurance policy receives the proceeds when you die. In naming a beneficiary you are not restricted to people; you can name a corporation, a charity, or even a pet. You can also have more than one beneficiary, who may share the proceeds equally or in any predetermined ratio. In general, you have the right to change your beneficiary as often as you wish.

What happens if your beneficiary dies first? You can name a new beneficiary, of course, but suppose you are unable to. For example, you have designated your wife as beneficiary, and both of you are killed in an accident, but she dies first. Now the money from your life insurance policy goes to your estate and is subject to probate fees and other costs before your heirs get it. To avoid this, you are permitted to name *contingent* beneficiaries, who will receive the proceeds if your first named beneficiary dies before you or if you both die in a common accident.

The money available from your insurance policy can be taken as a lump sum or can be paid in a variety of other ways. The types of *settlement options* include:

1. Lump sum. Your beneficiary is paid the face value of policy.
2. Interest only. The insurance company holds the money in the name of your beneficiary and pays the interest only on the sum.
3. Specified periodic payments. The company pays a fixed predetermined amount at regular intervals as long as the money lasts (plus accrued interest on unpaid amounts).
4. Periodic payments for a fixed time. The number of periodic payments is specified. The size of each payment is determined then by spreading the total amount available over the number of payments. Interest is added on unpaid amounts.
5. Life payments. The amount of each payment is based on the proceeds available and the life expectancy of your beneficiary.

You may select any of these options before you die and may change the designated option as often as you wish. If you do not select an option, your beneficiary may make the choice when the money is due. Although there may be a slight tax advantage to your beneficiary to have you select an option beforehand, it is usually impossible to tell what your beneficiary's needs will be at the time of your death. Thus, most people do not specify an option in their policies and leave it to their beneficiaries to do so. Unfortunately most beneficiaries select the lump sum payment because they do not know that other options are available.

The proceeds from your life insurance policy are not subject to income tax, but this money may be taxable as part of your estate. It is possible to avoid the estate tax if the policy *belongs* to your beneficiary. To accomplish this you must make your beneficiary the *owner* of your policy and give up all rights of changing beneficiaries. You may continue to pay the premiums. There are certain legal problems involved if the named beneficiaries die before you or if your wife is the beneficiary and you divorce. Therefore, it is well to seek legal advice before making your beneficiary irrevocable.

PROVISIONS AND FEATURES

Before you buy any policy, you should read it carefully to make sure no surprises are hidden in the fine print and to learn what your rights and privileges are under the policy. Most companies are reliable and do not put in clauses limiting their liability to obscure and unlikely circumstances. However, you should be aware of what companies do offer and make sure the company will give you the features you want.

A *grace period* of about 30 days is usually specified in the policy. Remember that the company can cancel the policy if you don't pay your premium, but the grace period allows you to be late without this risk.

The right to *change beneficiary* should be written in the policy. If, however, for the reasons stated in the preceding section you wish to make your choice of beneficiary irrevocable, then you do not need this provision.

Misstatement of age should not be grounds for cancellation of the policy. There should be a statement in the policy to the effect that if the age has been misstated, the benefits accruing shall be such that the premiums paid would have purchased at the correct age.

You cannot expect to buy a policy and have the company pay off if you commit *suicide* the next day or the next week. But what is a reasonable time beyond which the company cannot say you bought the policy with the expectation that you would commit suicide? This is usually specified in the policy and is typically two years.

Automatic premium loan is a feature of policies having cash value. This provides that if you do not pay your premium within the grace period, the amount of your premium will automatically be borrowed from the cash value of your policy. If you do not want this to happen, you must notify the company in writing. Since term insurance does not have cash value, this feature is not included in term policies.

Make sure your term policy is *renewable*. You may also wish it to be *convertible*, although this is something you can live without if you have a good savings program.

Disability waiver of premiums provides that if you are totally disabled, you no longer need to pay premiums, and your insurance remains in force as if you were still paying. There is an additional charge for this provision. Although the charge is usually very slight, there is some question whether this provision is desirable. If you become totally disabled, you need more than waiver of premiums. You need some source of income. Consequently, you probably will buy some sort of disability insurance to provide an income if you are physically unable to earn a living. The disability waiver of premium provision on your life insurance policy then becomes unnecessary. However, if the rate is very low, you might want to add it to your policy, but it is not a substitute for disability income insurance.

The life insurance policy is a contract that cannot be cancelled by the company after a stated period of time, even if you withheld pertinent information when you bought the policy. Normally, after two years the policy becomes *incontestable*. This must be stated in the policy.

As indicated in the section on beneficiary, you should designate a contingent beneficiary. If both you and your immediate beneficiary die in the same accident, the company would pay your contingent beneficiary regardless of who died first. The statement of this provision in the policy is called a *common disaster clause*.

A *double-indemnity* provision entitles your beneficiary to double the face value of the policy if you die in certain types of accidents. Double indemnity is usually quite cheap, but if you have adequate insurance, why spend money on a gamble? It is better to use the extra money for additional savings.

MAIL-ORDER INSURANCE

Like almost everything else, insurance can be purchased by mail. Some insurance companies do all their selling through advertisements in newspapers and periodicals and claim to give more insurance for your premium dollar because they don't have to pay salesmen's commissions. Most mail-order companies, whether they sell insurance or other commodities, are trustworthy but a few dishonest or unreliable companies tend to give mail-order selling a bad name. If you buy from a well-known established company, you can do well buying by mail.

Before you buy life insurance by mail, ask to see a sample policy. Check this policy to make sure that it covers the kinds of risk that you are interested in. If the policy covers only accidental death, for example, it is not sufficient for your needs.

Check with your state insurance commissioner to make sure the company selling the insurance is licensed to do business in your state. Even if it is not so licensed, it can still sell insurance through the mail. When a company is licensed in your state, the insurance commissioner wields some control over the way it does business and can help if the company and you or your beneficiary disagree.

In general, life insurance offered by mail does not require a physical examination. Insurance companies offering this type of insurance spread the risks by offering the insurance to a large group. Further, in the application you must indicate all the medical attention or treatments you have had in the past five or more years and must also state that you are in good health. If you then die from a condition for which you had been treated and failed to mention, your beneficiary will not be able to collect.

The premiums for mail-order insurance may be deceptively low, but read the fine print to make sure that the rates will stay low. If the company has the right to raise the premiums arbitrarily do not buy the policy. Low rates do not mean the company is dishonest, but to stay in business a company with very low rates must reject most claims.

Many companies use terms which lead the unwary to believe that the United States Government is offering the insurance, but unless the advertisement or policy specifically states this, do not be misled by false inferences. For example, "low-cost Military Life Insurance Policy" or "Special Armed Forces Policy" are **not** offerings of the Federal Government. The U.S. Government does in fact include life insurance among its benefits for veterans, but the policies are clearly marked as being issued by the Government.

SOCIAL SECURITY

A very important part of your life insurance program is *Social Security*. The amounts that are deducted from your paychecks are really premiums for an endowment life insurance policy. Both the amounts that are deducted and the benefits have been increased steadily and will probably continue to be increased in the future. In case of death of the insured, there is a small lump sum payment for funeral expenses. This was $255 in 1973.

The endowment feature of your social security insurance provides for monthly payments for you and your dependent spouse. If you live to 65 and are covered by social security, you will be paid a specified monthly income for the rest of your life. Your dependent spouse, if over 65, will receive a monthly income 50% of yours. Note that if a woman becomes 65 and applies for social security benefits, her dependent children under 18 then also receive monthly benefits. Also your children who are full-time students receive benefits until they are 22.

If you should die before 65, your widow (or dependent widower) will receive monthly benefits if she (he) has children under 18. If not, she will receive regular monthly benefits when she is 65. In all cases, a man can elect to receive reduced benefits when he is 62, and a woman when she is 60.

If you continue to earn a living after age 65, your benefits are reduced. However, interest, dividends, rents, royalties, and other "unearned income" are not considered when calculating your benefits. After age 72, your monthly payments are paid in full, regardless of how much you earn.

If you become totally disabled so that you cannot earn a living at any age, you will start to draw the same monthly benefit you would receive at age 65. If you have children under 18, your dependent spouse and these children also receive monthly benefits.

In order to qualify for benefits, you must have worked in some occupation covered by social security a certain minimum length of time. Almost any kind of occupation is covered, but if your income is derived from dividends, capital gains, and the like, you will not be covered.

You will be fully insured and eligible for retirement if you worked 40 quarters (the equivalent of 10 years) in occupations covered by social security. Once you are fully insured, you will be entitled to benefits on retirement (or your widow will on your death) even if you do not work for several years. If you are not fully insured, you are still entitled to a minimum benefit if you work for 1-1/2 years in the 3 years before you die or retire.

Anyone over 65 who is qualified to receive social security payments is also entitled to medical benefits under the Medicare program. This program pays most of your hospital bills. For a small monthly fee most of your medical fees will also be paid. It is probable that the Federal government will offer some kind of national health program covering all workers and their families in the near future.

Chapter Three

Savings Accounts

If you put $25 into a cookie jar every month, at the end of a year you would have saved $300. In five years you would have $1500. Now although this shows that appreciable amounts can be built up from relatively small contributions, everyone knows that a cookie jar is not the proper place for a savings account. Disregarding the possibility of loss by theft, you know that your money should earn more money in the form of interest, without the least risk. For example, if you put the money in a savings account that paid 5% compounded daily, you would have about $308 at the end of a year and more than $1700 in five years.

Five percent, compounded daily, is one of many different interest rates available as of this writing. Before you open a savings account, you should know what rates are available, and other pertinent facts concerning your account. *Don't be afraid to ask questions.* When you want to borrow money from a bank or other financial institution, you are subject to a barrage of questions to determine if you are a good credit risk. When you deposit money, you are in effect lending money to the institution, and you should be just as careful as the bank is.

An important reason for building up a savings account is to provide a fund for emergencies or for large future expenditures, such as a college education for your child or a protracted pleasure jaunt around the world. Many people, however, find it extremely difficult to maintain the discipline necessary to save. Such a person may honestly intend to start a savings account with his next paycheck, but somehow the temptation to spend the money is too great. Some may even take the first steps and actually start savings accounts, only to withdraw the funds whenever appreciable amounts have been saved.

Because many would-be savers lack the necessary discipline, most banks have set up special accounts with names like "Christmas Club", or "Vacation Club." These may seem attractive, but they are advantageous only to the banks. If you open such an account, you are *required* to make regular deposits or pay a penalty. Fear of paying the fine usually provides the needed discipline to make you save regularly. These "clubs" are poor ways to save. Most pay little or no interest. In addition, when the money is released, the depositor usually spends it too freely. Saving toward a vacation or for Christmas expenses is a laudable goal, but you can do much better in a regular savings account than in a club.

If you have the discipline to make yourself save, your only problem is where to put the money for maximum return and safety. But how do you force yourself to make regular deposits when you don't have to and how do you avoid the temptation of withdrawing the money? If you are faced with these problems, you have to practice a bit of self-deception. One method that works for many who lack discipline is to open a savings account and authorize the bank to transfer funds from your checking account to the savings account regularly. You deposit your paychecks in your checking account as you always do, and the bank writes a check against it regularly for the amount you want to save. This check is deposited in your savings account. Since you never see the money, you are not tempted to spend it. You can even use two banks, since you can authorize the bank where you have your checking account to make the savings deposits in another bank.

It may be easier for you if you have two savings accounts. Use one for short-term goals such as next summer's vacation or a color TV, and use the second for long-term savings like a college education for your child or a retirement fund. You can then tap the short-term account as needed or as tempted, but you do not touch the long-term account until the funds are required for the designated goal. The two accounts can be in the same savings institution, but it is probably easier to avoid temptation if they are in two different banks.

There are many methods of *compulsory* savings. Most large companies provide a method of payroll deductions for various savings plans, such as credit union deposits, U.S. Savings bonds, or stock in the companies themselves. If you sign up for one of these, the amounts are deducted from your paycheck, just as taxes are, and since you never see the money that is deducted, you do not have the temptation to spend it. Regular mortgage payments and life insurance premiums also possess the qualities of systematic savings since a portion of the payment is used to build up equity in your home or cash value in your policy. (Note: if you are buying term insurance as recommended in the preceding chapter, your insurance payments will include deposits to a savings account to build up a "cash value".)

TYPES OF "BANKS"

There are many different types of institutions that provide savings accounts, and not all of them are *banks* in a strict legal sense, but most people lump them all together as "banks". The important types are:

Commercial banks   These are the only ones that provide checking accounts and also offer the greatest number of financial services. They are authorized to make all types of personal and business loans.

Mutual Savings Banks   As the name implies, these banks provide savings accounts, but no checking accounts. They are restricted to lending their funds for mortgages and home improvement loans. Most states do not have this type of bank.

Savings and Loan Associations   Strictly these are not banks. This type was formerly called a building and loan association and was conceived as an alliance where members could pool their money to lend to other members for the purpose of building homes. Now S & L's lend money to non-members for home mortgages.

Thrift and Loan Associations   These are not banks, but associations of members who pool their funds to make personal loans.

Credit Unions   These are associations of people with a common interest, such as employees of one company or members of one club. The members buy shares in the credit union, and the funds are used for personal loans to members.

All of these institutions will gladly accept your money and pay you interest for using it. In effect, they lend out the money and pay you a share of the profit. In addition to "banks", you can save your money by buying U.S. bonds and notes. The important criteria for choosing a particular institution or a particular type of account are:

1. *Safety.*
   Will you lose your money if the bank fails?
2. *Availability.*
   How fast can you get your money if you need it?
3. *Amount of interest.*
   This involves the interest rate and the method of compounding it.
4. *Convenience.*
   Is the bank close to your home or business, and does it have suitable hours?
5. *Free services or gifts.*

SAFETY

In 1932, more than 2000 banks failed in the United States, and depositors in these banks lost all their savings. As a result two government insurance programs were initiated to protect depositors in the event of bank failures. Deposits in banks are insured by the Federal Deposit Insurance Corporation (FDIC); and those in S & L's by the Federal Savings and Loan Insurance Corporation (FSLIC). Both of these are federal agencies and are as reliable as the United States government. When these insurance programs were inaugurated in 1934, savings were covered up to $2500. Before the end of the year, the coverage was raised to $5000. The ceiling was raised to $10,000 in 1950, to $15,000 in 1966, to $20,000 in 1969, and to $40,000 in 1974. If your bank is insured by FDIC and fails, the money in your account, up to $40,000, will be repaid to you by FDIC. Although stricter requirements on banks and S & L's have reduced the number of failures, some do close their doors. Thanks to FDIC and FSLIC, their depositors do not lose their funds. When the United States Bank of San Diego, a billion-dollar institution, failed in 1973, the FDIC quickly and quietly paid off the depositors.

In 1932, one bank failure immediately precipitated runs on banks across the country, as the public hastened to withdraw their savings before their own banks failed. In some cases, the run on a bank caused it to fail. In contrast, the 1973 bank failure was accepted with apathy since the public knew that the FDIC would make good.

In the preceding paragraph, note the provision, "If your bank is insured—". Most banks and S & L's do have this insurance, but about 3% of commercial banks and S & L's, and a larger number of savings banks are not insured. When you select a bank or Savings and Loan, make certain that your account will be insured by the appropriate federal agency. This is usually indicated by the agency seal affixed to the window or door of the bank or S & L.

When the FDIC was first formed, bank accounts up to $2,500 were covered by insurance. This upper limit has been raised now to $40,000. What if you have $45,000 in a savings account and the bank fails? You would get back $40,000, and would lose $5000. The way to avoid this difficulty is to put your funds in more than one account. For example, you can have an account of $40,000 in each of five S & L's or banks, and if all of them fail, you would get back your $200,000. If it is inconvenient to use more than one institution, you can still be protected for larger amounts by using a variety of accounts, and each would be insured to $40,000.

An *individual account* is in the name of one person only. Although anyone can make deposits to the account, only the named individual can withdraw funds. If this person should die, the funds become part of his estate.

A *joint account* is set up in the names of two or more individuals. Normally, each may make withdrawals without consulting the other or others. However, the account can be set up to require two or more signatures for withdrawal. If one of the *joint tenants* should die, the funds belong to the survivors.

A *revocable trust account* is set up in the name of a *trustee* for the benefit of a *beneficiary*. Frequently, the trustee is a parent and the beneficiary a child, but other combinations are possible. Only the trustee may withdraw funds. If the trustee should die, the funds belong to the beneficiary.

Using these types of accounts, a married couple can open five accounts in one bank and have their funds insured to $200,000, as follows:

1. An individual account in the husband's name.
2. An individual account in the wife's name.
3. A joint account in both names.
4. A trust account in the husband's name for the benefit of the wife.
5. A trust account in the wife's name for the benefit of the husband.

If the couple has a child, the variations on trust accounts increase. In addition to the five accounts mentioned, they can have an account with the husband as trustee for the child, one with the wife as trustee for the child, one with both spouses as trustees for the child, one with the husband as trustee for the wife and child, and one with the wife as trustee for the child and husband. That's another $200,000 of protection. However, if anyone has $200,000 in savings, there are probably better places for part of the money than savings accounts.

The FDIC and FSLIC are equally reliable and cover commercial banks, savings banks, and savings and loan associations. Thrift and loan associations usually pay higher interest rates than banks or S & L's, but their funds are not insured by an agency of the federal government. Many of the T & L's belong to associations to which they contribute funds to cover losses from failures. In effect they have formed their own insurance company which insures the savings of depositors in member T & L's. In the unlikely event of a nationwide epidemic of bank failures, it is conceivable that the funds accumulated to cover failures of T & L's might not be sufficient to cover all the accounts of depositors in these associations, but as a practical matter, savings accounts in T & L's are relatively safe.

Credit unions use their funds for personal loans to members. If debtors default, a credit union loses money, but this risk is minimized by careful credit checks. Before 1971, the money in an account in a credit union was not insured, and thus these organizations were not as safe as banks, S & L's, and T & L's. Congress set up a credit union insurance program which went into effect on January 1, 1971. It is mandatory for federally chartered credit unions and optional for those licensed by states. It also set up strict specifications that credit unions had to meet within three years to qualify for the insurance. Unfortunately most did not in 1971 and some went out of business. The rest of the federally chartered unions did improve their operations and have qualified. Most of the state licensed credit unions do not qualify and do not carry the insurance. A few that could qualify do not carry the insurance because they must pay for the cost of the insurance. Only a small percentage of state licensed credit unions offer this insurance protection. A well run credit union can yield much higher returns than other savings organizations since the profit belongs to the members. Unfortunately most credit unions are run by the members themselves who are not necessarily experienced in financial matters, and as a result high returns on deposits are the exception rather than the rule.

However, those credit unions that offer savings insurance must be well run to qualify for the insurance and will probably yield better returns than those lacking insurance protection. If you put your savings in a credit union, you should make certain it is insured, both for the protection of your savings and for the assurance that the credit union is operated professionally. As more and more savers seek out only institutions offering insured accounts, other institutions will be forced to shape up and enroll in the insurance program to meet the competition.

U.S. Savings bonds and U.S. Treasury notes are as safe as the government itself. When you purchase a bond or note from the government, you are lending money to the United States for which you will receive interest on your money. Terms of these government obligations run from 90 days to 10 years.

AVAILABILITY

Next to safety, the most important requirement for your savings account is being able to get your money when you need it. When you deposit money in a savings account, the financial institution presumably lends the money to someone else at a higher rate of interest so that it can make a profit. If the bank, S & L, or other financial institution has idle deposits lying around not earning interest, it represents a potential loss since the institution must still pay interest to its depositors. It is easy to conceive then that if you walked into a bank and asked for some of your own money, that the bank might not have the funds readily available and would have to ask you to come back at a later date. In fact, if you read the fine print on the deposit agreement you sign when you open an account, you will learn that you are required to give at least 30 days notice if you want to make a withdrawal. This time interval gives the institution time to call in the funds from one of its outstanding loans.

In practice, you can get your funds immediately from most savings accounts. Banks, S & L's, and T & L's pay on demand. So do well-run credit unions. Some of the smaller credit unions do not have funds readily available and may ask you to wait, but the waiting period will be a day or two instead of a month. Of course, if every depositor in a bank wanted money at the same time, the bank might not have enough ready cash available and would then impose a waiting period. The 30-day period written into the agreement is to protect the bank against such runs as occurred in the 1930's, when fear of a bank failure precipitated a run which caused an otherwise sound bank to fold. However, since the advent of savings insurance, the public no longer fears bank failures, and runs are unlikely. In the course of a normal business day, a bank will receive funds from depositors and from payments on its own loans, and can use these funds to pay any depositors who want to withdraw funds.

Although you can withdraw your money immediately from most savings accounts, you should note that you may suffer some loss of interest when you do. This is discussed in the next section.

INTEREST

The amount of money that a financial institution pays you for the use of your money can vary widely from one bank to another and is different in different cities. You must consider how to get the best return on your money.

In times when money is short, all the financial institutions have more loan applications than they can handle. They must compete for the depositors' money and offer all sorts of inducements. If there were no restrictions on the amount of interest they could pay, they might well be willing to pay 10% or more interest on deposits and charge 18% for mortgages. The federal government would like mortgages to be available at reasonable rates and one way to control mortgage rates is to limit the interest a savings institution can pay on deposits. The maximum rate of interest that can be paid is set by federal regulations, but financial institutions don't have to pay the maximum. In areas where competition for the depositors' money is non-existent, interest rates on deposits may be well below the maximum.

The maximum rate of interest on savings deposits varies with the type of institution, the type of accounts and even with geography. In the early 1970s, commercial banks in California could pay 5% interest on ordinary passbook accounts, S & L's could pay 5.25%, and T & L's could pay 6%. Credit unions also offered 6%, but frequently added premiums of a share of the profits. Other special accounts in banks, S & L's, and T & L's carried interest rates up to 8%. Maximum rates in other parts of the United States were higher where capital was in short supply and lower where money was plentiful.

The amount of interest you receive on your deposit is dependent not only on the interest rate but on the method of compounding. If you deposit $1000 at simple interest of 5%, at the end of a year you receive $50 in interest. If the interest is compounded semiannually, you receive half of this interest or $25 at the end of six months, and at the end of another six months you receive not only $25 interest on the $1000, but also 62 cents interest on the $25 which was paid at the end of six months. Instead of $50, you get $50.62. Similarly, if the interest is compounded quarterly (every three months), at the end of a year you will get $50.94. If the interest is compounded every day, you will get $51.27. Note that with daily compounding, a 5% rate yields effectively 5.127% annually. In advertising for depositors' dollars, financial institutions stress the "effective annual yield". This is related to the actual rate, compounded daily, as shown in Table 4.

Before banks had computers, the task of calculating interest on deposits was laborious, and most banks compounded quarterly. Some still do, although with computers the job is greatly simplified, regardless of the compounding interval. A proper question to consider is whether daily compounding at a certain rate is better than quarterly compounding at a higher rate. If you put $1000 in each of two savings

TABLE 4 Interest Rates Compounded Daily

Annual Rate Compounded Daily in %	5.00	5.25	5.50	5.75	6.00	6.25	6.50	6.75	7.00
Effective Annual Yield in %	5.13	5.39	5.65	5.92	6.18	6.45	6.72	6.98	7.25

accounts, one at 5% compounded daily and the other at 5.1% compounded quarterly and left the money there for five years, the amount in each account at the end of each year is shown in Table 5. These are practically the same, but Table 5 does indicate that daily compounding is worth only an extra 0.1% of interest when compared to quarterly.

Equally important to you as a depositor is the method of bookkeeping used by the savings institution in calculating interest in an account where you might make occasional withdrawals. Regardless of the frequency of compounding, institutions usually pay their interest quarterly; typically on the last business day of March, June, September, and December. Some pay interest only on money still on deposit on those days. These institutions should be avoided. If you deposited $5000 on April 1 in such an account and then withdrew $4000 on June 15, you would receive interest only on the $1000 remaining on June 30. Look for institutions which advertise *"interest compounded daily, paid from day of deposit to day of withdrawal"*. If you put your $5000 in this type of account on April 1 and withdrew

TABLE 5 Comparison of Interest Compounded Daily and Quarterly

At End of Year	1	2	3	4	5
5 Percent Compounded Daily	$1,051	$1,105	$1,162	$1,221	$1,284
5.1 Percent Compounded Quarterly	$1,052	$1,107	$1,164	$1,225	$1,288

$4000 on June 15, you would receive interest on $5000 for 2-1/2 months and on $1000 for the last half a month, when the interest payment was made on June 30. In other words, as long as you have a minimum deposit (usually $5) left in your account on the interest-payment date, you will receive interest for every dollar that was in your account at any time in the last quarter and for every day it was there.

Federal regulations do allow financial institutions to pay higher rates of interest on certain special accounts. If you are willing to deposit your money for a specified period of time and will not make withdrawals, you can purchase a *certificate of deposit*. Strictly speaking you do not open a savings account, instead, you and the financial institution enter into a contractual agreement whereby you lend the institution a sum of money at a specified rate of interest to be paid back at a designated time. Certificates of deposit are available at banks, S & L's, and T & L's. As of this writing, S & L's in California are paying 5.25% compounded daily on passbook accounts and are permitted to issue certificates of deposit as described in Table 6. You must put up at least $1000, but there is no maximum. Each account is insured up to $40,000. The annual rate depends on the term as shown in the first two columns of Table 6. Since interest is compounded daily, the yield shown in the last column is somewhat higher than the designated rate. Some T & L's issue 8% certificates in minimum amounts of $5000 and with a term of three years.

Note that although a certificate of deposit enables you to get a higher interest rate, it does limit the availability of your funds. You can always withdraw your money at any time, but if you withdraw early, you must pay an interest penalty. However, you will always get back at least as much as you put in.

TABLE 6   INTEREST YIELD FOR CERTIFICATES OF DEPOSIT

Annual Yield	Time in Years	Minimum Amount	Annual Rate
7.5 %	4	$1,000	7.79%
6.75	2½	$1,000	6.98
6.5	1	$1,000	6.72

In an ordinary passbook account, you make deposits and withdrawals as you wish, with no loss of interest. With a certificate of deposit, withdrawals are prohibited, but you can deposit additional funds. When you do, the term for all the funds in that account begins over on the date of the latest deposit. To prevent this from happening, it is better to get a new certificate of deposit, either in another financial institution or by using joint or trust accounts in a slightly different arrangement.

A *bonus* account is a regular savings account with a slight resemblance to a certificate of deposit. A typical bonus account pays an extra 0.5% if you do not make a withdrawal for 90 days. For example, in an S & L the regular passbook account may be paid interest of 5.25%. When you open a "90-day" account, you will get 5.75% if you don't make a withdrawal for 90 days After the 90-day period, the money draws 5.75%, and withdrawals are permitted. Bonus accounts usually require minimum deposits of $500.

Interest on savings accounts has varied in the past and will vary in the future. When housing construction decreases, there is less demand for mortgage money, and lenders lower their rates in order to compete. They then have less profit to pay for the money they have on deposit. When you open a regular passbook account, there is no guarantee that the financial institution will continue to pay its current rate. On occasion depositors have been pleasantly surprised when interest rates were increased, but decreases can also occur. If you have a bonus account, the interest rate could also fluctuate, but the bonus is guaranteed. That is, if the bonus is specified at 0.5%, interest on bonus accounts will remain 0.5% higher than on passbook accounts. The certificates of deposit, however, have guaranteed rates. No matter how the regular interest rate varies, the financial institution will pay the interest specified on the certificate of deposit for the entire term of the contract.

United States Savings bonds are safe, but their interest rates are lower than those available in banks and other financial institutions. In fact, if you cash a bond before maturity, you will receive less than the expected yield.

When you have $40,000 in your savings account the interest added each quarter brings the total above the insured savings maximum. In case of failure, the FDIC or FSLIC would pay you $40,000, but you would lose the interest. You can arrange with the financial institution to have them mail you an interest check each quarter or even each month. In this way, the value of your account never exceeds $40,000. Most financial institutions provide this service on all savings accounts and certificates of deposit. You don't have to have $40,000 in your account to avail yourself of this service. If you have $1000 in your account and want to receive regular interest checks, the financial institution will be happy to oblige. Note, however, that you lose some of the effect of compounding, because when the interest check is mailed to you, you will no longer get interest on this interest. For example, a 6.5% certificate of deposit with interest compounded daily earns 6.72% in a year. If you elect to receive interest checks monthly, your yield will be about 6.6%. That is at the 6.5% compounded daily for one month.

United States Treasury notes are issued usually in $10,000 denominations and are short term, usually 30 to 90 days. Occasionally, $5000 notes may be available. Interest yields vary, but are generally higher than are paid on long term certificates of deposit. If you purchase a 90-day note at 9% yield, at the end of three months your money will have earned interest at the 9% rate, but you must now reinvest or redeposit it. If interest rates have remained high, you can purchase a new treasury note and still get a good rate, but if interest rates have dropped in the interim, you might find that you could have done better by putting your funds in certificates of deposit. If you have $100,000 or more available you should be looking at other modes of investment than savings deposits. Tax-free municipal bonds, for example, may yield less, but after taxes you might keep more.

HOW TO GET MORE INTEREST

All sorts of tricks and gimmicks have been devised to enable the depositor to get more interest than the maximum allowed by federal regulations. Not all of them are legal. A few representative ones are described here, but before adopting one of these, study it for pitfalls.

One method, which is apparently legal, is to have the bank act as a broker between you as a lender and someone who wants to borrow money. The borrower is usually a business. The bank in this case has no available funds to accommodate the borrower, and would dearly love to get hold of the funds you want to deposit. You then put your money in a certificate of deposit in the bank. The bank then lends the money to the borrower at its usual rate *plus an extra one or two percent for you.* The extra amount is negotiable and depends on how badly the borrower needs money. Your money in the certificate of deposit is insured (up to $40,000). Although, you are receiving extra interest, this extra amount is not paid by the bank. As long as the bank's payment to you does not exceed that allowed, the transaction is legal.

The maximum interest that a bank can charge a borrower is usually fixed by usury statutes, but in many states there is no minimum rate. If the officers of a bank saw fit, they could lend you money *at no interest.* This is the basis of another plan to enable you to get a higher rate of interest than the law allows. Assume you have $10,000 you want to put into savings. The bank can lend you, say $2000 at no interest, and you add this to your own money and put the $12,000 into a certificate of deposit. You draw interest on the whole $12,000, and thus in effect you get 20% more interest on your own money. This is legal, but the FDIC and FSLIC frown on it. If the bank should fail, the FDIC may refuse to make good on the grounds that you and the bank conspired to evade the maximum interest rule.

Many financial institutions pay interest from the first of the month on any deposits made by the tenth of that month, provided the money is not withdrawn before the end of the quarter. This suggests a method of getting extra interest that is perfectly legal.

On the tenth of January withdraw all but the required minimum from one account and deposit this money in another financial institution. Make sure both institutions pay daily interest. Assume you had $5000 in the first institution, and on January 10, you withdrew $4995 and deposited it in a second institution. You leave five dollars in the first account to make sure that you will receive interest on the $4995 up to January 10. In the second institution, your $4995 draws interest from the first of January. In effect then you receive an extra ten days interest on your money. Since the money must remain in the second account to the end of the quarter (March 31) to get interest for the extra ten days, you do not touch it until April 10. At that date, you withdraw all but $5 from the second account and deposit it in the first. By doing this every quarter, you can get an extra 40 days interest a year. Is it worth the effort? If you were able to get 6% in each account and were transferring $5000 each time, you would earn an extra $33 per year, or about eight dollars each time you made the change. To get this, however, you have in effect tied up your money for a year. You could do better by investing in a certificate of deposit.

CONVENIENCE

This is an obvious consideration, but of less importance than the others. Financial institutions maintain regular hours which usually coincide with the business hours of the shops and offices in their immediate vicinity. If these hours are inconvenient for you, you should look for a savings institution that is open on Saturday morning, some evening or whatever other hours suit you. Because of competition, many S & L's and a few banks are open at odd times to suit the person who cannot take time out during the regular working day.

Also, the institution should be conveniently located. If you have to drive many miles every time you want to make a deposit or withdrawal, or if you have to pay a parking fee every time you visit, your car expenses will offset any extra interest you might get.

Many institutions have solved the inconvenience problem by permitting banking by mail. When you open an account in one of these institutions, you are given a postpaid reply envelope and some form of deposit and withdrawal ticket. To make a deposit, you simply place the checks, a deposit slip, and your passbook in the envelope and mail it. The institution pays the postage. When the deposit is received, it is credited to your account, and your passbook is returned by mail along with a new deposit slip and a new postpaid reply envelope. Withdrawals are made in the same manner, the institution mailing you a check in the amount of your withdrawal. The main advantage is that you can make the deposit or withdrawal when the saving institution is closed. Also, since you need not visit the premises, you can bank wherever you can get the best interest, even in another state. One disadvantage is that you should not deposit cash, since it is inadvisable to send cash through the mail. Another is that you must wait for the return mail when you make a withdrawal.

FREE SERVICES

When competition for depositors' dollars became hot, S & L's gave free gifts to anyone who opened an account. It was not unusual to see an advertisement offering a gift worth $50 to anyone who opened an account with a minimum of $1000. This represented an extra 5% return. The regulatory agencies took a dim view of this practice and finally ruled that an S & L could spend no more than $2.50 for a free gift. Theoretically, it is possible for an S & L to purchase more expensive manufacturers' close-outs at $2.50 each and give them as gifts, but in practice the new rule effectively ended the flood of free gifts available for depositors.

To attract depositors, S & L's began offering free services, and since the services that an S & L can offer are limited, practically all offer the same things. These include free money orders, free notary service, free safe-deposit boxes, free travelers' checks, free trust deed collections, and free checking accounts. The checking account is in an associated commercial bank, since S & L's do not offer checking accounts. If you need any of these services, make sure your S & L offers it, since it does represent additional income in the form of saving money you would otherwise have to spend.

WHICH INSTITUTION?

Banks still charge for services and offer lower interest rates than S & L's. Thus, it is difficult to see why anyone should use a bank for a savings account when an S & L is available. There is little difference among S & L's, and you may choose one on the basis of personnel. Although T & L's and credit unions do not usually offer free services, they do pay a higher interest rate and are therefore attractive.

There is some move toward unification of the different types of financial institutions. It is expected that in the near future, laws will be passed permitting all of them to lend money to the same types of borrowers and to pay the same interest on deposits. All will offer the same types of accounts including interest-paying checking accounts as well as savings accounts.

Chapter Four

Checking Accounts
and Charge Accounts

A checking account in a commercial bank enables you to write checks to pay your bills. A charge account enables you to purchase goods and services to be paid for at some later date, usually by check. Checking accounts and charge accounts are totally different things, but they do have similar effects on your savings. When used properly, they can increase your interest income; when used improperly, they can be very expensive.

CHECKING ACCOUNTS

When you open a regular checking account in a commercial bank, you receive a supply of blank checks and deposit slips. Every month the bank mails you a statement showing the checks that you have written, the deposits that you have made, and the balance in the account. The bank also returns your cancelled checks which you can save as proof of payment of your bills.

The bank pays no interest on the money you have on deposit. Indeed the bank may even charge you for each check you write and each deposit you make, unless you maintain a specified minimum balance, typically $300. If you are a good customer for some of the other services provided by the bank, you can usually get them to waive the minimum balance requirement.

You can get blank checks with your name and address printed on them *free of charge*, but this is not publicized. When you open an account, you are offered a choice of checks in a variety of fancy designs and sizes and pre-numbered, for a slight extra charge. Unless you want the prestige of a fancy check, it is pointless to spend money on these. The checks that the bank furnishes free are just as reliable for payment and as proof of payment. It is not too difficult to number each check as you write it instead of having the checks pre-numbered. Also, if you make an error in writing a check, you can tear it up without a qualm when your supply is free.

Banks sometimes offer a variety of services for a flat monthly charge which varies from bank to bank, but is typically about two dollars. Included in these services is a checking account with no minimum balance requirements. It would seem that $24 a year is too much to pay for these services since almost all of them can be obtained free at S & L's and elsewhere. If you wanted to maintain a minimum balance of $300 in your checking account, you would get this service free also, and the interest you lose by not putting the $300 in a savings account is less than $24.

Banks have added what at first glance looks like a benefit, but is actually a very costly privilege when you are not careful. Formerly, if you overdrew your account, the bank would return your check marked "insufficient funds". Now most banks allow you to overdraw your account up to an amount determined by your credit rating. This is typically $1,000. Why are they so generous? Because they charge you interest on the amount overdrawn until you repay it. The interest rate is about 1.5% a month, or 18% a year! At this rate, they hope you never repay the overdraft. In fact, if you simply deposit a sum in your checking account sufficient to cover the overdraft, the bank ignores it and still charges you interest. They can do this because when the overdraft occurred, they automatically issued you a loan to cover it at 1.5% a month. This is a separate transaction from your checking account. In order to stop making additional interest payments on the loan, it is necessary for you to designate that your new "deposit" is not for your checking account, but is to cover the loan. Nevertheless, this service can be valuable. If you suddenly have to make a large purchase, you can write a check without worrying that the check will bounce. Just make sure to repay the loan as quickly as possible.

If you write only a few checks a month, you may want a *special checking account*. With this type of account you don't have to maintain a minimum balance, and you pay a flat rate for each check you write. Thus if you write only five checks a month, your cost will usually be less than one dollar. This is better than maintaining a minimum balance of $300, since your $300 in a savings account should earn more than one dollar per month. However, if you arrange for a free checking account through your S & L, you might do better. If you only write two or three checks a month, you don't need a checking account. With a savings account, you will not be reprimanded if you make a withdrawal every week, and the withdrawal can be in the form of a check made out to whomever you designate. You can also use the free money orders offered by your S & L.

Since no interest is received on deposits in a checking account, it is foolish to keep a large balance there. If the minimum balance for free service is $300, and if your checking account balance is always at least $1000, you are losing the interest on the $700 that could be in a savings account. Ideally, the amount in your checking account should be slightly more than the minimum balance. When you have to write some checks, transfer sufficient funds to cover them from your savings account to your checking account. If you write frequent checks, however, you should make only one transfer a month to cover them, since the bother of making the change is not worth the saving in interest. A $500 balance is $200 over the minimum, and $200 would earn only about one dollar per month interest in a savings account.

NEGOTIABLE ORDER OF WITHDRAWAL

It would be nice to be able to get interest on the balance in your checking account. After all, the bank has the use of your money and should be willing to pay for it. From the bank's standpoint, the checks issued to you, monthly statements and service, constitute payment. Some S & L's have developed what is called a Negotiable Order of Withdrawal or NOW account which is essentially a checking account that draws interest. Since S & L's are not supposed to offer checking accounts, commercial banks are understandably up in arms. To understand how a NOW account works, first consider a simpler account S & L's have developed for your stock market purchases.

Millions of people invest in common stocks and bonds through stock-brokers. When they sell stocks, most of these investors leave their money with their brokers until they make their next purchase. At any one moment, there are hundreds of thousands of dollars in brokerage houses, credited to customers' accounts but not drawing interest. For a long time financial institutions tried to devise a method to obtain the use of these idle funds, and some S & L's have finally found an answer. If you are dealing with a stock broker, you open a special savings account in an S & L and authorize your broker to withdraw funds from it to pay for stocks you buy. When you sell a stock, your broker receives the money for it and immediately deposits it in your savings account. Instead of having idle cash in your account at the broker's office, where it draws no interest, your cash earns interest in your savings account between investments. Interest is paid from day of deposit to day of withdrawal and is compounded daily. This concept is simple, but basically it is not new. You have always been able to authorize someone else to withdraw money from your savings account.

If you can write an authorization for someone else to withdraw a specific sum of money from your savings account, why not make this authorization transferable? Then the person you authorize can in turn authorize another. In other words the withdrawal order is *negotiable*. In practice, the NOW looks like a check. The person you authorize is the payee. He in turn authorizes another by "endorsing" the authorization. The endorsement can be to bearer just as with an ordinary check. In effect, a NOW account is a checking account that pays interest.

Many banks are vociferously opposing NOW accounts at this writing, but it is unlikely that these accounts will be eliminated. More probably, some arrangement will be worked out so that banks and S & L's both will be allowed to offer checking accounts that pay interest.

CHARGE ACCOUNTS

It's nice to be able to buy now and pay later. It's also risky because there is too much temptation to buy more than you can afford. Yet if you can avoid this temptation, being able to buy on credit has many advantages.

Not too long ago the best credit risk was the person who paid cash for all purchases. With the advent of computers, the cash purchaser became a nonentity whose name and address were not needed or known to the seller. On the other hand, the charge customer's purchases and payments were carefully recorded. If the payment came in at a reasonable time after the purchase, the charge customer received an excellent credit rating. Most stores favor their charge customers, giving them advance notice of special sales and making it easier for them to return or exchange purchases.

Charge purchases broadly speaking include all purchases of goods or services for which the customer pays at a later date, either in a lump sum or in installments. There are different types of accounts and different methods of payment, and it is important for you to know how much you pay for the privilege of buying on credit.

Telephone and utility services are usually bought on credit. That is, you make your phone calls and use gas and electricity at your convenience, and you don't have to pay for these services until you get your monthly bill. If you pay these charges before the due date indicated on the bills, there is no interest charge. But note that if you fail to pay in time, you will be charged interest as much as 1–1/2% per month or 18% a year. You will also be threatened with termination of service. Despite the fact that the telephone is handy, most people do not make unnecessary long-distance calls, yet these same people yield to the temptation of abusing their other charge accounts.

Most department stores and specialty shops have a variety of charge accounts with fancy names. They all boil down to two methods of payment. If you pay the entire amount due before a specified date (typically, 30 days from date of bill), you pay no interest charge. If you leave a balance due, you pay interest on the unpaid balance which can be as much as 1–1/2% per month.

Single-use credit cards are issued by gasoline companies and some department store chains, such as Macy's and Penney's. These are really ordinary charge accounts but the credit card identifies you as a customer and lets you make charge purchases in areas outside your home city or state where you might otherwise find it difficult to provide identification. Again, if you pay on time there is no interest charge.

Multiple-use credit cards can be used in almost any establishment that offers credit. These cards are of two kinds. The *bank credit cards*, such as Master Charge and BankAmericard, are free, but you must establish that you are a good credit risk to get one. You can usually do this by opening a checking account in a participating bank or by having other charge accounts with stores or oil companies. *Entertainment cards*, issued by Diners Club, Carte Blanche, and others, require an annual fee for using the card. You must also establish your credit to get one of these cards. For most people, a bank credit card covers all normal requirements, and the fee for an entertainment card would be wasted. If you travel widely, however, you may find use for an entertainment card and should consider what it covers that is not covered by a bank credit card. As with many other charge accounts, you can pay your credit card bill completely before the due date and incur no interest charge. If you make a partial payment, you will be charged 1—1/2% per month on the unpaid balance.

Note that a credit card is the equivalent of cash, and should be guarded like cash. If you lose a credit card, the finder can make unlimited purchases with it. However, if you notify the issuer of the card (bank, oil company or department store) promptly, your liability is limited to $50 per card for fraudulent charges made prior to the notification. For a fee of about five dollars a year it is possible to buy insurance to cover all fraudulent charges on all your credit cards in case of loss.

Think of your credit card as money. Whenever you are tempted to make a charge purchase, imagine that you are taking money from your checking account to pay for it. With this in mind you may be able to resist the temptation to make unwanted charge purchases.

Installment buying is another form of making charge purchases. When you buy on the installment plan, you agree in advance to pay a portion of the amount at prescribed intervals, usually monthly. The interest is added to each monthly payment. Homes are almost always bought on the installment plan, and frequently automobiles are too. The true interest rate must be specified. It is usually higher than is apparent at first glance. For example, assume you buy something that cost $500 and pay $100 down. You agree to pay the $400 balance plus $32 interest in monthly payments for 12 months. This amounts to $36 per month. Since $32 is 8% of $400, you might think you are paying 8% interest, but actually you are paying approximately 16%. This is so because you do not owe $400 for the whole year, but as you pay off the debt, the average amount you owe during the year is $200. Thus, $32 is 16% of $200. If you must buy on the installment plan, make sure you know the true interest rate. It might scare you enough to ask yourself if the purchase is really necessary.

Rather than buy on the installment plan, you might be able to borrow money at a lower rate than the true installment rate. Commercial banks and credit unions lend money for personal loans. If you have a life insurance policy with a loan value, you can borrow money against the policy from the life insurance company at a very low interest. In any case, you borrow sufficient funds to meet your bill when it falls due, and then repay the loan in installments at the reduced rate. If this sounds too easy, don't be tempted to fall in the same trap of buying things you can't afford just because you can buy them on credit.

Despite its hazards, a credit card or charge account is a desirable convenience. It enables you to take advantages of legitimate sales when you are short of cash. For example, your black-and-white TV set is on its last legs, and your local department store is offering a color TV at a discount of $150. You are temporarily short of cash but the opportunity is too good to miss, so you buy the set and charge it. By the time you have to pay the bill, you will have the money. Even if you drag out the payments for two or three months, the interest you pay on the unpaid balance will be small compared to the savings you got by buying at the sale price.

There is a small but real financial gain you can achieve by buying as much as possible on credit. Assume that you regularly spend an average of $100 a month on goods and services you could charge. This could include drugs and prescriptions, gasoline, airline tickets, hospital bills, department store goods, theater tickets, hotel bills and even plumbers' bills. All of these and many more may be charged on a bank credit card. It takes an average of two or three weeks before you get the bill for the charged items and then you have about four weeks to pay the bill. By leaving the $100 in your savings account for an extra six weeks instead of paying cash, you gain the equivalent of six weeks interest for each monthly bill of

$100. This amounts to about eight or nine dollars for the year. This might seem like a trivial amount, but the important point is that using charge accounts doesn't cost you a thing, and it does give you the advantages of being a favored customer and establishing a good credit rating.

TRUTH IN LENDING

The true rate of interest that you had to pay when you bought any-thing on the installment plan was once a dark mystery. Sellers could add a service charge as well as interest to the price and in this way bypass usury laws. Advertisements might state "only $10 down" or "$20 a month," but fail to state for how many months payments had to be made. Then in 1969 the Truth in Lending Law went into effect. The purpose of this law is to let consumers know exactly what the real interest charge is on installment charges, mortgages, loans, credit card and other charge purchases. Further, the law specifies a uniform format that creditors must use when they state the charges, so that purchasers do not have to wade through fine print to find out what the charges are.

The total cost of borrowing money (whether on a loan or buying on credit) must include the interest charged plus any service charge or carrying charges. Under the law, all these costs must be added and the sum stated as a *finance charge*. The finance charge can be expressed as a percentage, such as 1–1/2% of the unpaid balance per month. In addition, the *annual percentage rate* must be stated. When the finance charge is a monthly rate, the annual percentage rate is twelve times the monthly rate.

Note that the Truth in Lending Law does not set a maximum finance charge. Most states have usury laws establishing a maximum rate, and these laws apply. The Truth in Lending Law simply enables the consumer to learn easily what rate he is paying.

The Law also regulates the advertisements of credit terms. If a business advertises one feature of its credit, it must mention all important details, including the down payment, the number of in-stallments, the amount of each installment, and the period of payment.

Another important provision of the Truth in Lending Law is

to protect the homeowner from high pressure salesmen for home improvements. If your home needs a major repair job, you may be required to give the building contractor a lien on the house to assure him of payment. If payment is to be in installments, the lien remains until the last installment is paid. Under the law, if you enter into an agreement in which your home is to be used as collateral, you have three business days to think things over and cancel the agreement by notifying the creditor in writing. Note that this right of cancellation does not apply to a first mortgage when you buy a home.

The law also provides criminal penalties for willful violation. It also enables the debtor to sue any creditor for failure to disclose the finance charge in the required manner.

Chapter Five

Automotive

Next to your home, your biggest expense is probably your car. If your only consideration were transportation, it would be easy to approach the problem of buying and maintaining a car with common sense. However, the automobile manufacturers and their advertising agencies would have you believe that a car is a status symbol and that if you do not own the latest creation, your neighbors will look down on you; your children will suffer untold embarrassments, and your social life will be curtailed. Unfortunately, after being exposed to this type of advertising for more than 50 years, the people have come to accept it as fact. Thus there are emotional and psychological factors involved in owning a car, as well as economic considerations. If you can see through the automobile manufacturers' propaganda, you will be able to consider your car strictly on a dollar and cents basis, even if you have to impress business clients who believe this propaganda.

DEPRECIATION

Of all the expenses of owning a new car, the largest is *depreciation*. Depreciation on a new car begins the moment you drive it off the dealer's lot, and in the first year amounts to one-fourth to one-third of the price, depending upon the popularity of the particular make and model. If a car is in demand, it will depreciate less than other cars of the same type. Thus, a one-year old Cadillac is worth more than a one-year old Chrysler, even though both might have had the same original price when new. Similarly, a Ford station wagon depreciates less rapidly than a Ford sedan. If you plan to trade in your car every year or two, depreciation is an important consideration. Although future rates of depreciation cannot be guaranteed, the past history of the depreciation of the particular make is the only guide you have for the coming years. Table 7 shows possible values for a popular car and one that is just as sound mechanically, but not as prestigious.

The values in Table 7 are approximations since the true value of a car is what you can get for it depending on condition, mileage, and time of year, as well as make, model and age. However, using Table 7 as a guide you can see that if you wanted to trade in your car at the end of two years, you would be $400 ahead with the popular model. Actually this is true only if you sell your old car yourself and then buy a new car without a trade–in. When you trade your old car for a new one, the dealer may give you an inflated allowance, but without a trade-in he would have reduced the cost of the new car from the sticker price. This Table is not to be taken as an indication of the car's worth, but rather as evidence of the expense of depreciation. If you buy a popular $6000 car, at the end of a year it has cost you $1500 in depreciation whether you drive it or not. If you drive about 10,000 miles a year, the cost is 15 cents a mile for depreciation in addition to costs of gasoline, oil, insurance, and maintenance.

Manufacturers of popular cars like to call attention to their high resale value compared to the average cars. This is another way of saying the popular car depreciates less rapidly. However, when a car is more than five years old, its mileage and condition are more important factors than its make and age. A *well maintained* automobile should give very little trouble for about 100,000 miles, or about ten years of driving for the average family.

TABLE 7   AUTOMOBILE DEPRECIATION

	Popular Model	Ordinary Car
New Price	$6,000	$6,000
One Year Old	4,500	4,000
Two Years Old	3,700	3,300
Three Years Old	3,200	2,850

MAINTENANCE

In addition to the expense of gasoline, oil, and routine lubrication, maintenance includes repairs or replacements of defective parts. Although modern cars are engineered to go 100,000 miles or more, individual parts wear out and must be replaced. Thus, a set of tires may be good for 40,000 miles, spark plugs for 15,000 miles and a battery for three years. The useful life of other parts is harder to predict. On some cars a thermostat or a water pump may last ten years, while on others these and other small parts will have to be replaced in three. Even if you buy a new car every other year, you will be lucky if you do not have any maintenance problems.

The need for maintenance must be considered from two viewpoints. First the inconvenience of unexpected breakdowns, and the nuisance of not having your car available when you need it. The second is the cost of repairs. These two considerations are not necessarily related. When you buy a new car, you can expect frequent maintenance problems during the first year. These are in the form of minor adjustments and repairs that crop up for two reasons. First, the new cars today are coming off assembly lines so fast that they are not completely checked before shipment. Second, there is a certain amount of "wearing in" during the first few thousand miles of driving a new car, requiring the tightening of bolts and nuts and other small adjustments.

There is usually no cost for these repairs in the first year, since the car is covered by the manufacturer's guarantee. After these minor adjustments have been attended to, you should expect a new car to require no maintenance for two or three years, except for periodic lubrication.

As a car gets older, repairs and replacements are needed more frequently. You need a new battery, new spark plugs and new tires. The fan belt is worn and should be replaced. Water hoses become dry and brittle. With a little care and preventive maintenance you can avoid the unexpected breakdown. Parts rarely stop working without prior warning. Every time your car is brought in for routine lubrication and oil change, you should check all parts that may wear out. If you replace defective parts instead of trying to get the last extra mile out of them, you may spend a bit more money, but you'll avoid the surprise breakdown. The cost of maintaining your car increases with age until the car is about five years old and then remains fairly constant for the next five years. This happens because owners of older cars do not spend money on purely cosmetic repairs such as a dented fender, or on maintaining the car for quick getaways or high power. The cost of keeping an older car *reliable* remains constant until the car needs a major repair such as a new transmission or motor. When this occurs, it's time to look for another car.

Other Parts The components of a car do not usually cease working without some warning signals, but you have to check for these signals. Thus, a battery does not suddenly go dead. Long before its demise, a simple battery check would have shown the existence of leaking cells or other signs that the battery was on its last legs. Every time you have your car lubricated, you should include a battery check in the process. Similarly, check all hoses and the fan-belt for wear or stiffness. Your owner's manual lists the parts that should be checked or replaced at a certain specified mileage. If you do not have a copy of the manual, send to the manufacturer for one. It is an important tool in keeping your car in good operating condition. As the car gets older, you tend to get lax, about changing sparkplugs, for example, but if you want to avoid unpleasant surprises treat your old car as you would a new one, and follow the recommended maintenance procedures. You will be rewarded with thousands of miles of trouble-free travel.

INSURANCE

You don't have to insure your car in some states, but it is unwise not to do so. If you have an accident, you can lose your license unless you can prove financial responsibility. An insurance policy is considered proof. Without insurance, an accident subjects you to liability which may exceed all your assets. There are several basic types of automobile insurance to be considered. The most common are:

1. *Liability insurance* pays for damage to others for which you are liable.

2. *Comprehensive coverage* pays for damage to your car from theft, fire, vandalism, and other assorted causes.

3. *Collision insurance* pays for repairs to your car if it is damaged.

4. *Uninsured motorist coverage* pays for your own injuries when the other driver who would normally be liable flees the accident or is unable to pay.

5. *Medical payments insurance* pays medical bills for yourself and your passengers, regardless of who is responsible.

6. *Road service insurance* pays for towing and emergency road service.

Of these, liability insurance is the most important and should be considered a necessity. There are two separate components to liability insurance: *personal injury* and *property damage*. The personal injury coverage is usually expressed as two numbers such as 10/20 or 100/300. The first number is the amount in thousands of dollars that the insurance company will pay to one person for personal injuries as the result of an accident. The second is the maximum that the company will pay for any one accident. Thus, 10/20 means that the company will pay up to $10,000 to one person and up to $20,000 for one accident. Since juries have been awarding huge damages to people injured in auto accidents, you should not skimp on your liability coverage. It is wise to buy 100/300 coverage which in fact costs only a little more than 50/100. Certainly, 50/100 is the minimum coverage you should have. Property damage coverage can be as low as $10,000, and $25,000 is more than sufficient—unless you intend to smash up a $60,000 Rolls Royce.

Comprehensive insurance is comparatively cheap and should be bought for cars up to about five years old. Older cars are rarely stolen. If your car is old and has a low value, you don't need comprehensive insurance, but because it is very cheap you may want to buy it anyway.

Collision insurance is comparatively expensive. It reimburses you for repairs on your car even if you drive it into a wall. Even if your car is new, you should not buy collision insurance. Over the years you will save enough to buy several cars. If you should be so unfortunate as to have an accident causing heavy damage, you can get partial redress by deducting most of the loss on your income tax return, even if you do not have the car repaired. If you have an accident where the other person is at fault, his insurance will cover your damages. The moral is: Drive carefully and don't buy collision insurance.

Uninsured motorist and medical payments coverage are relatively inexpensive. You may buy them for peace of mind.

Road service coverage costs less than a membership in an automobile club and covers much the same kind of emergency road service. The auto clubs, however, do provide other services, such as free maps and trip planning. If you have occasion to use these, join a club instead of buying this insurance.

Insurance for compact cars is cheaper than for large cars. The cost of comprehensive insurance is less for older cars than for new ones. You can also get discounts on your liability insurance by maintaining records as a good driver and, with some companies, by being a non-drinker.

Many states have enacted "no-fault" insurance laws, and eventually all states will have them. This type of law provides that if a person is injured in an automobile accident, all his medical expenses will be paid by the insurance company regardless of who is at fault. Before "no-fault" insurance, an injured person could collect only if he proved the other driver was at fault. This usually resulted in costly litigation to establish blame. As might be expected, trial lawyers oppose "no-fault" insurance.

Where "no-fault" laws have been enacted, insurance companies may pay more claims, but at a lower cost than litigation. As a result, automobile insurance rates have decreased in states having no-fault insurance.

FINANCE CHARGES

It is always cheaper to pay in full for your car, but sometimes it is necessary to buy on the installment plan. It is wise then to shop around for the cheapest loan. Financing the car through the dealer who sold it to you may be the most expensive. Regular commercial banks will usually finance your car at a lower net cost. The cheapest financing available is probably from a credit union, but you must be a member. The savings in interest charges by financing through a credit union rather than a dealer can amount to 10% of the loan.

Since you can avoid finance charges by paying cash, it is wiser to plan to drive your old car another year and start a savings account ear-marked for a car purchase a year hence. In effect you make the installment payments to your savings account until you have enough to buy the car you want. If you continue paying these installments to your savings account after you buy the car, when the time comes to get another one, you will have amassed enough to pay in full again.

NEW OR USED?

There is no doubt that it is more economical to buy a used car than a new one. If you buy a car two or three years old, you avoid a huge depreciation expense. Try to find one of the *less* popular models that depreciates more rapidly the first two years. You will pay less for it, and it should be just as good as the popular make and give good service. After the second year, depreciation on a car is moderate. Insurance costs are also less for an older car. Maintenance costs are higher for a used car, but are far less than the amount saved on depreciation.

Maintenance is the biggest bugaboo for most people who are considering buying a used car. The reasoning seems to be that if the car were in good condition, the previous owner would not want to get rid of it. Therefore, any used car is apt to break down unexpectedly and repair bills could be enormous. This reasoning may apply in a few cases, but most cars two or three years old have many years of useful life in them. The unexpected breakdown is rare if the car is checked thoroughly at the time of periodic lubrications. When you buy a used car, get hold of an owner's manual for that model and follow the manufacturer's recommendations on regular maintenance.

For the most economical and trouble free transportation your choice should be a car two or three years old and you should plan to drive it until it has gone about 60,000 miles. After about 60,000 to 70,000 miles the car will still be economical, but trips to the service garage will be more frequent and more inconvenient. If you can tolerate some inconvenience, there is no reason why you cannot drive your car 100,000 miles or more.

When you buy a used car from a private party, you should ask to make a road test. Ideally you should have the car evaluated by your favorite mechanic, but there are things you can check yourself. If a car two years old has a new paint job, forget it. New paint on a car less than three years old usually covers signs of an accident. Avoid any car that has been in a serious collision. Make all the obvious checks: door handles, switches, locks, window cranks, seat adjustment levers, and the like. Look under the car for leaks. Check brake action. Look for unusual wear on pedals, suggesting excess mileage. Make sure the odometer works, and that the mileage reading is correct. In most states, tampering with the odometer is illegal. Start the engine and listen for unusual noises. Race the engine, and see whether blue or black smoke comes out of the exhaust, a sign that the car burns oil.

Now drive the car. The transmission should work smoothly with slow acceleration, both forward and in reverse. Accelerate rapidly to 50 or 60 miles per hour. There should be no jerking, stalling, or sputtering. Apply the brakes at various speeds. The car should stop without pulling to one side. Drive over a rough road to check the comfort factor.

If a car pleases you, but has a few minor faults, figure out what it would cost you to repair it and mentally add this to the cost of the car. If the total is not out of line, you might then be willing to buy the car.

You can look for bargains among the less popular cars. For example, if the depreciation on a Dodge is greater than that on a Pontiac, in models that sold for the same price originally, after two years the Dodge will be cheaper.

Used foreign cars are frequently quite inexpensive. The smaller foreign makes are economical to operate and reliable. However, when a new part is needed, it may take several days to get it, since parts for foreign cars are not always readily available.

If you must buy a new car because of job requirements or prestige, you will miss the economy of a used car. But do keep in mind that a used luxury car, such as a Continental or Cadillac, can be just as prestigious as a brand new Ford or Chevrolet, and may cost you less.

UPKEEP

A compact or sub-compact costs much less than a large, luxury car, and the upkeep for the small car is usually substantially less. Some of the larger cars with air conditioning and full power options may run only six miles on a gallon of gas, while sub-compacts get 25 or more miles to the gallon. If you drive 10,000 miles a year, you will use about 400 gallons of gasoline in the sub-compact, but more than four times as much in the luxury car. With gas at 50 cents a gallon, you would spend about $200 a year in the small car, $400 in a standard sized model, and more than $800 in a luxury car. On a mileage basis, gas costs 2 cents a mile in the compact, four cents in the standard, and eight cents in the larger car. Gasoline is one of the major automotive expenses.

If you have a periodic lubrication and oil change every 6000 miles (as recommended in owners' manuals) and pay about $25, your cost is less than 1/2 cent per mile. Even if you do this every 3000 miles (as recommended by mechanics), your cost is less than one cent per mile. Larger cars require more oil than the smaller ones.

A set of tires is more costly for the larger car. Typically, a set of tires guaranteed for 30,000 miles may cost $80 for a compact and twice that for a large car. Even at $160, this set of tires costs only about 1/2 cent per mile.

Insurance may cost from one to three cents per mile, depending on the age of the drivers and the use made of the car. Insurance is cheaper for a pleasure car than for one used in business. Smaller cars and older cars cost less to insure.

Table 8 summarizes the approximate costs per mile for upkeep of different size cars. To these figures you must add the cost of depreciation. During the first year the total cost of owning and operating a new car runs from about 11 or 12 cents per mile for a sub-compact to more than 40 cents per mile for a luxury model.

Although the small car is much more economical to maintain,

TABLE 8   UPKEEP COSTS PER CAR MILE

	Compact	Standard	Luxury
Gasoline	2 cents	4 cents	8 cents
Oil and Lubrication	¾	⅞	1
Tires	¼	⅜	½
Insurance	1	1¼	1½
Totals	4 cents	6½ cents	11 cents

it is definitely not as comfortable as a larger car. The compact is ideal for driving to and from work and for shopping, but it is not recommended for long trips. Salesmen and others who use their cars for traveling great distances need a larger, more comfortable car. However, if you plan only one long trip a year, you can get by with a compact for your usual driving. Then *rent* a larger car for your vacation. You will find it cheaper than owning a larger car all year long.

TIRES

For safe driving, tires should have a tread of at least 1/16 inch in depth. The tread grips the road when you brake and keeps you from skidding when the road is wet. Because it is dangerous to drive on tires with worn treads, manufacturers have built wear indicators into their tires so that smooth narrow bands appear across the face of the tire when the tread is less than 1/16 inch deep. In most states it is illegal to drive on tires worn beyond this point.

When your tires are worn and must be replaced, which type of tire should you buy? The old, conventional bias tires are available with rayon, nylon, or polyester cords and are guaranteed for 18,000 to 24,000 miles. Belted bias tires have two or more belts added between the tire body and the tread. These belts may be made of fiberglass, rayon, or steel. Belted tires are guaranteed for about 30,000 miles. Radial tires are constructed differently, and also have belts. They may be guaranteed for 40,000 miles.

As you might expect, radial tires are the most expensive and bias tires the least. From the standpoint of miles per dollar, bias tires are somewhat cheaper, but there are more important considerations. Bias tires tend to squirm and run hotter than belted bias or radial tires. The squirm produces more wear. Radial tires have a larger contact area and thus offer better handling and more control in steering and stopping. Radials also improve gas mileage slightly. Note that radials should not be mixed with other tires, and tires on any one axle should always be the same. You may have radials on all four wheels, but never on one, two, or three wheels. Belted bias tires on all four wheels give better control and handling than four bias tires. If you use two belted and two bias, put the belted tires on the rear wheels and the bias in front.

If your car is to carry heavy loads, you may want to buy a larger tire than was on the car originally. However, make sure that the larger tire will fit in the fender well and will not rub on the under part of the car when the wheel is turned. Larger tires are also more difficult to steer, unless your car has power steering. Wider tires are also available for better cornering and control. They too are more difficult to steer and may rub against the underparts of the car.

Heat buildup in a tire not only can be dangerous but it also shortens tire life. Heat is caused by traveling at sustained high speeds, by overloading the tire, or by underinflation. At high speeds, the bias tires tend to run hotter than belted or radial tires.

If your driving is primarily short trips around town where you don't have to worry about heat buildup, a four-ply bias tire can satisfy your needs. Polyester tires cost more than nylon or rayon, but are worth the small difference. Nylon tends to develop flat spots when the car remains overnight. These are not dangerous and disappear after the car has been driven a few miles.

If you drive on turnpikes frequently, a belted bias or a radial tire is preferred. The tread should not be too thick, since tires with thick treads get hotter than those with thin. Your best buy here is probably a belted bias with a lower mileage guarantee, since the tread varies with the mileage. A high quality bias tire might be adequate but why take the risk? The belted bias does not cost much more.

If you plan to carry heavy loads, make sure the tires you buy are rated for the load. Note that you can increase the load capacity of your tires by increasing the air pressure, but only up to a point. For example, a common belted tire designated F78-14 will carry 1400 pounds when inflated to 28 pound per square inch, the recommended pressure. It will carry 1500 pounds at a pressure of 32 psi, which is the maximum safe pressure. Inflating the tire above 32 psi is dangerous. The maximum safe pressure is printed on the tire. The recommended pressure with normal loads is usually stated on a sticker on the door of the glove compartment. All pressures specified are to be checked when the tire is cold. For extra heavy loads, you may have to add heavy duty shock absorbers to your car.

Never buy a tire smaller than the original equipment. Note that four tires rated to carry 1400 pounds each will support a car and load weighing 5600 pounds, if the load is distributed equally. If you install a smaller size tire than needed for the load on that wheel, the tire will overheat.

Make sure your tires are kept at the proper pressure. Underinflation and overinflation both cause excessive wear, and underinflation also causes heat buildup which shortens tire life. Buy a pocket pressure gauge and check the tires about once a month when they are cold. Keep them at the recommended pressure with normal loads, and at the maximum permissible pressure when the load is heavy.

Have your wheels aligned and balanced at least annually. Improper alignment causes irregular wear on the front tires. This suggests that more even distribution of wear will occur if the tires are rotated. This is true, but if you have to pay to have the tires rotated, you will spend more for the rotation than you will save in extra mileage.

DEALING WITH DEALERS

There is a common belief that most car dealers, especially in the used car business are dishonest. This is far from true. In fact most car dealers are honest, whereas most car buyers have larceny in their souls. You, the potential buyer, know that the sticker price is just a formality and you try to talk the dealer into accepting as low a price as possible. Most buyers who trade in old cars tend to overrate their old models to such an extent that a casual eavesdropper might wonder why they want to get rid of such wonderfully reliable cars. Naturally the dealer wants to get as high a price as possible, but if he offers too little on a trade-in he is called dishonest.

A dealer does have an advantage over a potential car buyer. He is experienced in selling, whereas, the car buyer is not experienced in buying. He doesn't really have to use tricks and gimmicks in the bargaining process since he bargains every day, and it becomes second nature to him. From long experience he also is able to size up buyers and knows which ones can be induced to spend more than they want to or can afford. It is foolish for you to believe that you can outwit the dealers, but there are some steps you can take to get the most for your money whether you are buying a new or used car.

One important consideration is timing. In the fall, after the new models have come out dealers are besieged with buyers who have waited for the latest cars. From a financial viewpoint this is a bad time to buy since dealers have more than enough business and don't have to make concessions to get sales. The best times to buy are when sales are slow and dealers are worried about staying in business. At these times, especially if they have large inventories of unsold cars, they will accept any *reasonable* offers to move cars off their lots. At the end of the summer, a few weeks before the new models arrive, dealers are sometimes frantic to get rid of their stock of new cars. If you want to buy a new car and not pay for the first year's depreciation, this is the time to buy. But beware! The new car is a one-year old-model and when you want to trade it in later, it will be one year older than the car you would be able to buy in a few weeks. If you trade every two years or so, you can't really gain by buying these year-end-model bargains. If you plan to hold the car for five years or longer, then you really save the first year's depreciation. The end of the summer is also a good time to buy a used car from a dealer. He knows that when the new models come out, he is going to do a lot of business, and practically all of his customers will have old cars to trade in. He wants to clear out his used car lot to make room for the flood of trade-ins he will be getting in a few weeks. He can do this by wholesaling all his cars to special dealers who buy cars in huge quantities at low prices and sell them in a state where used cars are scarcer. In the meantime, he will try to sell off as many as possible at prices which are bargains to the purchasers but still more than wholesale.

There are two other times of the year when sales are slack and bargains are available. In December, people are preoccupied with the coming Christmas and its attendant expenses. They do not have spare cash or credit available to spend on a car. Automobile dealers offer more bargains to promote sales. A similar situation exists in February in areas where winter weather is unduly harsh. People don't want to buy new cars when there is much snow on the ground. As at the end of the model year when new car sales are slack, so are used car sales.

When you are about to buy a car, new or used, decide what style and how much you will spend before going to any dealer. Too often, the buyer comes in to a dealer's showroom expecting to buy a serviceable used car and is shown the latest shiny models in new cars. The dealer or his salesmen emphasize how much better the new car is than the older models, and the customer falls in love with the new model. As a result the customer spends more than he can afford. Dealers are well aware of the impact of a brand new car on the car-conscious buyers and will offer a few genuine bargains to lure prospective customers into their showrooms. For example, a dealer will advertise an excellent used car at perhaps $500 to $1000 less than the going price, knowing that it will draw many prospective buyers to his showroom or lot. Only one can buy the car, but many others who come to the lot will not go away without making purchases. A few disgruntled customers may accuse the dealer of dishonesty, but in fact he did have the car for sale and sold it as advertised to the first customer who wanted it.

In addition to knowing what you want and what you can afford you should know where to buy, especially, if you want a used car. In general, you should stick to established new car dealers who also have used car lots. An established dealer will be in business if you have complaints later. Also, he usually has the personnel and facilities for reconditioning the used cars he takes in trade. He will not try to sell the worst "dogs" he takes in, but will wholesale them to independent lots.

Unless you find exactly what you want at the price you want to pay, do some comparison shopping. Remember that the bottomline price is the important consideration. One dealer may offer you $500 for your old junk heap as a trade allowance on a $2000 car, while a second dealer realistically appraises your trade-in at $200 but will sell you the same make and model as the first at $1700. In both cases your net cost is $1500. Some buyers are apt to be impressed by the $500 allowance, but you should realize that both dealers are offering the same deal. In fact, the second deal will actually cost you less because you pay a sales tax on $1700 instead of $2000.

You may be able to realize a net gain by selling your old car yourself rather than trading it in. The dealer who takes your car in trade expects to sell it at a profit, so it might be possible for you to get a higher price than the trade-in allowance. However, this does involve the bother of advertising, showing your car to prospective buyers, and other inconveniences. You must judge for yourself whether the possible return is worth the extra effort.

Regardless of what kind of deal the salesman offers you and no matter how beautiful the car looks, insist on driving the car and making the checks mentioned in the preceding section, before you commit yourself. If there are faults that are easily corrected, you should try to get the dealer to include the needed repairs in the cost of the deal. Make sure all promises and guarantees are *in writing*. If a salesman promises that some corrections will be made but fails to give you a written statement to that effect, you may have no redress later. You may be told that the salesman who made those promises is no longer working for the dealer.

Whether you intend to trade in your old car or sell it yourself, you should put it in good condition to make a good impression on the dealer or buyer. This does not mean you should have extensive body work done to repair dents; nor should you give it a coat of paint. The possible increased return would not cover the cost of the body work or a paint job. But there are many things you can do at little or no cost which will enhance the value of your old car. Clean it. That is, wash the outside, vacuum the inside, and remove obvious spots on the upholstery with any spot remover. Clean the trunk and glove compartment. Touch up scratches and rust spots on the outside with touch-up paint. Check that the tires are at their correct pressure, and that fluid levels are correct in radiator, crankcase, battery, and all reservoirs. The object is to give the impression that the car is well maintained.

THAT SECOND CAR

Do you need a second car? Frequently when the family auto gets old, and the owner starts shopping for a car, he rationalizes that having a second car would be a convenience and would not cost much more to operate. Further, the amount to be realized in trade is too small to bother with, so he decides to keep the old one and pay cash without a trade-in for the new purchase, whether it is a new car or a more recent model. He figures that the old car costs practically nothing and that operating costs are the same whether the total miles are driven in one car or divided between two.

Before you fall into this trap, make sure you need the second car, because it is an added expense. Granted a second car is a convenience, but understand how much you are paying for that convenience, and then decide whether it is worth it. It is true that operating costs per mile may be no different if the mileage is divided between two cars, but a basic fact of life is that a family that has two cars, drives more than it did with one. As an average, when a second car is added, the family drives 40 to 50% more annually. Maintenance on the old car is also a factor to be considered. Insurance for two cars is not double, but is substantially more than for one. All these expenses should be added to the amount you could have realized by selling or trading in the old car to arrive at the real cost of owning a second car. If the added convenience is worth this expense, then you can own a second car.

If a second car is needed only part of the year, as when a teenage son or daughter comes home from college for the summer, you might do well to buy a junkbox that runs. You can frequently pick up an inexpensive car that looks bad but is serviceable for shopping trips. Then when your offspring returns to school, you can sell the car, sometimes for as much as you paid for it.

OPTIONAL EQUIPMENT

When you want to buy a new car, you will find that there is a base price for the car and then various charges for so-called *optional equipment*. Automatic transmission, air conditioning, power brakes and steering, radio and heater, and an assortment of interior decors are among the options. Actually these are not truly options since the cars that the dealer receives are already equipped with most of this extra equipment and he would charge as much to remove them as they cost originally. If a car is equipped with a stereo tapedeck and you want the car, you must buy it with the tapedeck. To be sure, you can put in an order for a car without the options and if you are willing to wait, you will get one eventually, but most people who intend to buy, make their purchases from what is immediately available in the showrooms.

The same thing can be said for used cars. If you want a car without air-conditioning, the dealer will not remove the air-conditioning apparatus from an auto in his used car lot. You can only choose from what is available and must realize there is nothing *optional* about this equipment.

The optional attachments add several hundred dollars to the cost of a new car. However, the options depreciate faster than the basic car. In the case of an older car, the condition of the car and the mileage are more important in determining the value than a full array of options. If you shop the less popular models of cars three or four years old, you will find you are paying very little for the optional equipment.

Beware of gimmicks! Many periodicals carry advertisements of devices to attach to your car to increase gas mileage. Most of these are worthless, and some actually increase gas consumption. You can be sure that if a simple device to increase gas mileage existed, car manufacturers would have incorporated it in their models years ago. It is true that in some cases you *may* increase your gas mileage by bypassing the pollution-control device on your car. However, this does not always work, and it is illegal and can subject you to a stiff penalty.

Chapter Six

Shelter

If you are like the vast majority of people in this country, your largest expenditure is for shelter. Whether you own your own home or rent, whether you live in a luxury apartment or a slum, housing probably takes more of your earnings than any other single expense. Yet unlike your other expenses, financial considerations play a minor part in your choice of a place to live. If you want to own your own home, whatever the reason, it is meaningless to ask whether it is cheaper or more expensive than renting. If you want a *decent* neighborhood for your family, it is pointless to consider an inexpensive flat in a slum district. If a yard for your children and a garden are important, you won't want to consider a suite in an apartment house or even a luxury hotel.

Nevertheless, the amount you can spend for a home is limited by your income and other expenses, and it is important to be able to weigh the pros and cons (including costs) of the various types of housing available. You may choose to live in an apartment, in one of a group of connected houses or in a duplex, in a single detached house, in a mobile home, or even in a houseboat. All of these are available either for rent or for purchase, although the types of housing facilities may be limited in any one locality. That is, a suburb may have restrictions on apartment houses, and a city may prohibit mobile homes.

Is it cheaper to buy or rent? This question has no satisfactory answer because it usually refers to owning your own single home versus renting an apartment. There are cheap apartments and luxury apartments, and likewise the cost of a new home can vary by a factor of more than ten. If you compare identical dwellings, one to be rented and the other for sale, it is usually cheaper to buy, since you save the landlord's profit. You will save some money buying a house rather than renting it. Similarly, you will find it less expensive to own your own apartment, rather than renting it. However, you cannot really compare an apartment with occupancy of a single house without considering many factors beside costs.

Some of the arguments in favor of renting a home are:

1. Rent is fixed. Thus you have better control of your expenses for housing.
2. You will usually spend less on decorations and furniture for a home you rent than for one you own.
3. You are not tied to a long term commitment. You can move when the lease expires. If you owned the house, you would have to find a buyer for the property. Renting is more flexible than ownership.
4. You have little responsibility outside of paying the rent. The owner is concerned with taxes, repairs, and maintenance, but you can lock the door and leave whenever you wish. If you own a home, you constantly have to attend to details of maintenance.
5. Renting allows you to build up a savings account.
6. Renting gives you a chance to learn what your housing needs really are without being tied to a house you may not want or in a neighborhood you may not like.
7. When your future housing needs are uncertain, renting is the best compromise.
8. You may be temperamentally unfit to cope with the problems of home ownership.

Some of the arguments in favor of owning your own home are:

1. Money put in a home is a good investment. If you buy with care your property will increase in value. In time of inflation, owning a home is a good hedge since you will be paying off your mortgage with inflated dollars.
2. The interest payment on your mortgage and your taxes can be deducted on your income tax return. In effect the government helps pay part of the cost of owning your home.
3. Owning a home forces you to save since you must meet mortgage payments. The amount paid toward the principal increases your equity in your home.
4. As your equity increases, your family will gain an increased feeling of security. A home that is completely paid for is a substantial asset.

5. A home provides a better environment for raising a family than an apartment.
6. Your credit rating is improved if you own your own home. You can borrow money for emergencies and for alterations without additional security.
7. Owning is more prestigious than renting.

RENTING AN APARTMENT

When you rent an apartment, you know exactly what your cost for shelter will be each month. There are no surprises. If the roof leaks or the plumbing is clogged, you simply call the owner of the apartment house or his agent, and the defect is fixed at no cost to you. The repairs may not be as perfect as they would be if you owned the property yourself, but they are usually adequate. Landlords are understandably reluctant to spend more than absolutely necessary to keep an apartment livable. For example, the owner may patch a leak in a pipe, rather than replace the pipe. But whatever problems arise, your cost is only the amount you pay for rent.

Apartment living usually means no yard or garden. There is no lawn to mow, no snow to shovel and no furnace to tend. There is a freedom from responsibility that you do not have when you own a house. If you want to go on a vacation, you lock the door and go. You don't worry about snow, grass, weeds in the garden or trash collections. For a young couple with no children, apartment living makes sense, especially if both the husband and wife work. For an elderly couple whose children have grown up, apartment living gives them the desired freedom from the responsibility of home ownership.

When newlyweds are about to move into their first home, they don't really know what they want in a house. Apartment living gives them a chance to find out, without tying themselves to a long term commitment. If you don't like your apartment, you can move. If you don't like the home you own, you have the problem of selling it before you buy another. Renting at the start also gives the couple time to look for just the right home to buy instead of having to choose from what is available at any one instant.

For the person of average means, owning a home may be more prestigious than renting an apartment, but in the upper income

Interior of a luxury apartment. *(Photo courtesy of Oak Creek Apartments, Palo Alto, Cal.)*

echelons, renting can be more glamorous. Luxury apartment complexes are available with all the amenities and facilities of a fine hotel. If you are willing and able to pay, you can have maid service, use of tennis courts, swimming pool, and many other facilities. Luxury apartments offer private meeting rooms for small conferences or large parties. You can entertain lavishly without even bringing your guests into your apartment. Some of these complexes include a variety of shops so that you never have to see the outside world. Needless to say, the rental cost is much higher than the cost of owning a home because you pay for all the services as well as for shelter, but if you can afford it, this is a pleasant life style.

RENTING A HOUSE

When you rent a single house, you have the advantage of a yard, and more space than you have in the average apartment. Although you

Luxury apartments feature excellent athletic facilities for physical fitness.
(Photo courtesy of Woodlake, San Mateo, Cal.)

are not responsible for major repairs, in most cases you do have to take care of the yard, shovel snow, and fix small things like a leaking faucet. You generally know what your monthly costs will be. It would probably be cheaper in the long run to buy the house. There are, however, legitimate reasons to rent. Your job may be temporary, and you expect to be transferred to a different city. You may not know what you want in a house and you prefer to rent one until you know your requirements. You may not have enough saved for the down payment.

When you live in a house, you usually interact with the neighbors, more than an apartment dweller. If you have children, they should have other children their own age to play with. Once the children get together, the parents are drawn together for children's activities such as scouting, and then mix socially on an adult level. The neighbors around you, whether owners or renters, are an important consideration in selecting a house.

It is usually a good idea to rent your first home, preferably with an option to buy. If you like it, you can take up the option later. In the meantime, you can "try it on for size". You will become acquainted with the area and the neighbors. You will learn if the house feels spacious or cramped. Remember, when children come, the house must be roomy enough for a larger family. Even though you don't pay for repairs, you will find out how frequently repairs have to be made and will learn something about their costs.

The same considerations apply to renting half a duplex or a flat in a two or three-family house. You will have a yard, though it will usually be smaller than that of a one-family house. You will have

Main pool area of a luxury apartment complex. *(Photo courtesy of Park Newport, Newport Beach, Cal.)*

The lounge in a luxury apartment is available for bridge games and private parties. *(Photo courtesy of Woodlake, San Mateo, Cal.)*

to know your neighbors, at least in the other flats in the house, since you will be sharing the yard and other facilities with them. You may not be required to mow grass or shovel snow, especially if the owner lives in one of the flats, but it is also possible that the tenants are expected to take turns at these chores.

COST COMPARISON

If the consideration is owning a house versus renting an apartment, cost comparisons means nothing, since other factors are more important. Before considering the factors involved in owning your home, it might be well to compare the cost of renting versus owning identical houses.

If you knew how much a house really cost, it might scare you away from owning one. Consider a simple $25,000 house. You pay

$5000 down and apply for a $20,000 mortgage. When money is scarce, lenders charge a fee for making a loan. This fee is expressed as points, where a point equals one percent of the loan. Fees range up to 3 points or 3 percent of the mortgage face value; although if you shop around, you should be able to negotiate a loan for a fee of one point. In the case of a $20,000 mortgage, this amounts to $200, which is paid in advance. Other costs paid in advance include appraisal fees, costs of checking the title, and other closing costs. The lending fee and all the costs of closing the sale might be $1000. Thus your initial out of pocket cost for down payment and closing fees amounts to $6000.

You are able to negotiate a $20,000 mortgage at 8–1/2% for 25 years. This will cost you $161 a month, which doesn't seem too high. But 25 years is 300 months, and $161 multiplied by 300 is $48,300. In addition your taxes, insurance, water, and maintenance may add up to about $1000 a year or another $25,000 for the 25-year period.

The total cost of your "$25,000 house" is thus 6000 + 48,300 + 25,000 or $79,300! This doesn't include the interest you could have gotten if you put the $6000 in a savings account and rented an apartment instead of buying. The actual cost of the house is more than *three times* the selling price.

Don't let this high cost scare you. If you wanted to rent the same house, it would cost you about $250 a month, or $75,000 for 300 months. At the end of 25 years, you would have spent less money than you would if you had owned the house, but you would have nothing but rent receipts to show for it. If you own the house, at the end of 25 years it is yours free and clear. You no longer have to pay $161 a month on the mortgage. If you continue to live in the house your monthly cost is less than $100 as compared to the $250 it would cost you to continue to rent. In addition, you have the security of owning an asset worth $25,000, which you can realize, should you decide to sell the house.

On the other hand, you must not forget the $6000 out-of-pocket expenses that you paid when you bought the house. Suppose that you decided to rent instead of buy. You would be able to put the $6000 in a savings account to grow at compound interest. At 7% compounded daily, you would have about $35,000 in your account at the end of

25 years. That is, you would have if taxes didn't take a bite of the interest. Each year, you would have to pay a portion of the interest to the government for income taxes. The amount you have left after taxes depends on your tax bracket, but could be $20,000 to $25,000.

Income taxes tip the scale slightly in favor of the homeowner. The interest on your mortgage and the amount paid for property taxes are deductible on your income tax return. The effect is that the government pays part of your expenses when you own a home. For example, the interest and taxes for the first year on your $25,000 home may be $2500, of which the government pays about $1000 (depending on your tax bracket). Over the years, the tax deductions add up to a sizable portion of the $79,300 cost indicated above. However, this figure also depends on the rest of your deductions. If you are married and file a joint return, you are permitted a $2000 standard deduction. If your actual deductions totaled only $1200, you could still claim $2000. Now if you buy a house and want to itemize deductions, you would claim the same $1200 plus the $2500 interest and taxes on your home. This adds up to $3700 which is only $1700 more than the standard deduction. The net effect is that your $2500 interest and tax expense buys you only a $1700 deduction on your return.

In the preceding discussions, it has been assumed that taxes, rent, and interest remain constant for the 25-year period. This is most unlikely. In periods of inflation, rents, taxes and interest rates increase. In periods of recession, rents and interest rates decrease, but taxes do not fall unless the recession is prolonged and severe. Over a 25-year period the economy will normally fluctuate quite widely, but the trend will generally be inflationary. The cost of living at the end of the 25-year span might be expected to be about three times what it was at the beginning. This does not mean that your $25,000 house will necessarily be worth $75,000, but it certainly will be worth a lot more than its original cost, despite depreciation.

For the renter, this means that rents will increase. Although you might still be able to rent something for $250 a month, it is unlikely to be as desirable as the house you rented at the beginning of the period. In fact, if history is to be a guide, rents have more than tripled in the quarter-century following World War II. Also, the interest you receive on the $6000 in your savings account will have less buying power than the same amount of money a few years earlier.

For the owner, inflation means your home will be worth more when you desire to sell it. Your interest rate remains constant for the term of your mortgage, which means you will be paying off your debt with inflated dollars. These dollars have decreased buying power for everything except paying off your mortgage. You can expect increases in taxes, insurance rates, and maintenance costs, but your mortgage payments remain constant. The net increase in cost of housing is substantially less than the increase in the cost of living.

BUYING A HOME

When you decide to buy a home, your first problem is to determine how much you can afford to spend. Various rules of thumb have been given. One typical rule is that your house should not cost more than twice your annual income. Another is that your housing expenses, after your down payment, should not be more than one-fourth of your income. Such general guidelines are usually meaningless. Much depends on the size of your income and the needs of your family. Thus, a buyer earning $15,000 a year might be hard-pressed to afford a $30,000 home, whereas the man earning $50,000 per year might be satisfied with a $50,000 house. Also, the amount you can afford to spend depends on the prevailing interest rates at any one time. When interest rates are high, the amount you have available for monthly payments will not buy as big a mortgage as during low-interest periods.

The first step is to determine how much you have available for housing. You must have sufficient savings for a down payment, with enough reserves for closing costs, moving expenses, and new furnishings that may be required. You then estimate all your *non-housing* expenses, including savings and recreation, and subtract this from your income after taxes. What you have left will have to cover mortgage payments, taxes, insurance, utilities, and maintenance. Maintenance can only be estimated, since you never know when you will need a new roof or other major repairs. Your available funds for a down payment and the monthly amount you can allot to housing determine the maximum price you can spend for a home.

Your best source of information on houses available for sale is a reputable real estate agent. In areas that have multiple listing, a seller places his home with one realty company, but all the real estate agents connected with the multiple listing group are apprised and given the opportunity to sell it. Thus, the agent you select when you want to buy a home probably knows about most of the houses offered for sale in your area. Any commissions are paid by the seller, so that using an agent costs you nothing. You should also check the newspapers for the few homes advertised by prospective sellers who do not want to pay the agent's commission. However, a reputable agent can save you a lot of running around by showing you only houses in your price range, in neighborhoods where you might be willing to live.

The one thing you cannot change in a house is location. Therefore, before you look at any offerings, you should first pick the areas in which you would be willing to live. You want a neighborhood that will fit in with your family's requirements, but you also want to have some assurance that the neighborhood will not deteriorate. Judging the future is always difficult, but here are some guidelines:

1. Check the zoning restrictions. A zoning map should be available for your inspection in city hall. An area limited to single-family homes with minimum lot sizes specified is preferred. It should be zoned against undesirable uses.
2. Note the availability of schools, shopping centers and public transportation.
3. Look at other homes in the neighborhood. Are they well kept or rundown? Do families live there for long terms or is there a large turnover? A stable population usually means that homes will be better cared for and that they will increase in value.
4. Are the homes connected to sewers or do they use septic tanks? If there are no sewers, you may have to face an assessment later when sewers are laid, but the value of your home should increase after being connected.
5. Does the area have adequate police and fire protection?
6. Are streets paved?
7. Are the houses of a convenient size for modern living? Old houses with many rooms require a staff of servants. These may be stately mansions, but because of the unavailability of servants they may be turned into rooming houses.
8. Do other families in the neighborhood have interests and incomes similar to yours?

9. Are there any objectionable noises (traffic, trains etc.) in the neighborhood?

When you are shown a house for sale in a desirable neighborhood, you have to judge if it is suitable to your family's needs. If this is your first home, you will not be a good judge, but here are some things to consider:

1. Size. Are there enough bedrooms? Are the rooms large enough for comfortable living? Is there enough closet space? Storage space?
2. Design. Is the house attractive and comfortable? Is it easy to maintain?
3. Privacy. This includes privacy from neighbors and individual privacy inside the house.
4. Construction. Check walls for cracks, floors for squeaks. After a heavy rain, check basement for dryness, roof and gutters for leaks. Check adequacy of plumbing, electric wiring, heating system, water pressure. Check for termite damage.
5. Lot. Grounds should be adequate for your needs. Landscaping adds value to the property. Check condition of lawn and trees.
6. Equipment. If stove, refrigerator, and other appliances are included in the sale, check to make sure they are in good condition.

In some states, a house must be inspected before it can be sold. The buyer normally pays for the inspection, but the seller pays for any repairs required. Even if your state does not require an inspection, it might be worthwhile to have it done. Your realtor should be able to supply the names of qualified inspectors.

Some of the best buys are old houses that are *not* in good condition. If you can buy one cheaply enough, the total cost including repairs will be less than the cost of a similar house in good condition. If you are handy with tools and paint, your savings can be tremendous.

When you have found the house you want, you will be required to sign a sales contract. This is an important agreement in which the conditions of the sale are spelled out. The contract should specify the purchase price, delivery date, details of financing, and that the sale is conditioned on your being able to get a loan and on the seller being able to deliver a clear title. If any furnishings are included in the selling price or any repairs are to be made before delivery, these should be itemized in the contract, and it should also state who shall pay for costs of repairs. It is usually wise to hire a lawyer to check the title to the property and to make sure that the sales contract contains all the terms and conditions satisfactory to both buyer and seller. In some states, the title must be checked and guaranteed by a title company.

After you have arranged financing and made your down payment, you will be given a deed to the property. A *warranty deed* gives the buyer title to the property. The seller warrants that it is a clear title. If it subsequently turns out that the title is flawed, the buyer can sue the seller for breach of warranty. In states with title insurance the buyer could collect damages from the insurance company, which presumably had checked the title before issuing the insurance. A *quit-claim deed* gives the buyer whatever rights the seller had, which may be nothing. When you buy, you should insist on a warranty deed or buy title insurance. The lender who finances your mortgage may insist that you have title insurance. Note that if a bank normally conducts its own title search before it will lend mortgage money on a house, you don't have to pay a lawyer to duplicate the effort.

Mortgages When you buy a house, it is unlikely that you will have enough cash on hand to pay for it. In fact, your available funds may only be a small part of the total purchase price. To make up the difference you must *mortgage* the house. A mortgage is a pledge of property to guarantee payment of a debt. When you mortgage your home, you are pledging it as security for the loan. If you fail to meet the terms of the loan agreement, the lender can *foreclose* the mortgage. That is, he can cause the house to be sold and then get back the amount due on the loan from the proceeds of the sale. You, the borrower, are the *mortgager*; the lender is the *mortgagee*.

Most mortgage loans are paid off in equal monthly installments for a specified number of years. The mortgage agreement should specify the amount of the loan, the interest rate, the monthly payment, and the number of payments. Other provisions may include prepayment penalties and privileges. At first, a large part of the monthly payment pays the interest on the loan, with the balance applied to paying off the principal. As the balance due decreases, the interest also decreases, so that a larger amount of each monthly payment is applied to reduce the outstanding balance.

The size of the monthly payment depends upon the amount borrowed, the interest rate, and the length of time it will take to pay off the loan. A low monthly payment is not necessarily desirable since you will be spending too much on interest.

The monthly payment for each $1000 of loan is shown in Table 9. For example, if you had a 20-year $20,000 mortgage at 8%, you would pay 20 × $8.37 or $167.40 each month for 20 years. Note that the longer the period of time for any fixed interest rate, the lower is the monthly payment. Also, the lower the interest rate is for any fixed time, the lower the monthly payment.

You will pay more total interest if you elect to pay over a longer period of time even though the monthly payments are smaller. Consider, for example, an 8% mortgage. If you pay in 20 years, you will pay $8.37 per month for 240 months, or a total of $2008.80 to pay off a $1000 loan. This means you pay $1008.80 in interest. If you pay in 25 years, you pay only $7.72 per month, but you pay it for 300 months. This is a total of $2316, about $307 more interest than for the 20 year loan. If you start with a $20,000 mortgage at 8%, it will cost you 20 × $307 or $6140 more to pay it off in 25 years than in 20. Now consider the effect of a lower interest. Again, the 8%, 20-year loan will cost you a total of $2008.80. If you can get a 7–1/2% rate,

TABLE 9 MONTHLY PAYMENTS FOR EACH $1000 OF LOAN

Interest Rate	Payment Period				
	10 Years	15 Years	20 Years	25 Years	30 Years
6	11.11	8.44	7.17	6.45	6.00
6½	11.36	8.72	7.46	6.76	6.33
7	11.62	8.99	7.76	7.07	6.66
7½	11.88	9.28	8.06	7.39	7.00
8	12.14	9.56	8.37	7.72	7.34
8½	12.40	9.85	8.68	8.06	7.69
9	12.67	10.15	9.00	8.40	8.05

you will pay $8.06 for 240 months, or a total of $1934.40, which is about $74 less than the 8% loan cost. For a $20,000 mortgage, you would save 20 × $74 or $1480.

Obviously, you should strive for the lowest interest rate and shortest time period you can get and still meet the monthly payments. Lenders worry about their money, and anything you can do to alleviate their fears will encourage them to give you better terms. If you make a large down payment, the loan is small compared to the value of the house, and the lender knows you are unlikely to default. You should be able to get a lower rate. Typically, in 1974 an S and L offered mortgage loans at 8-1/2% when a cash payment of 20% of the value of the house was put down, but lowered the rate to 8–1/4% when 25% down was paid. They also charged one point or one percent as a loan fee. If you put up about one-third of the price in cash and offer to pay in 10 years, you may get as much as 1% less than the current rate.

Mortgage rates vary over the years. In 1928, loans at 8% were common. During the depression years of the 1930's, you could get 4% mortgages with no down payments. Banks owned houses on which they had foreclosed the mortgages and were only too happy to be getting interest on them again. In 1950, you could still get a 4% mortgage if you shopped for it and made an adequate down payment. Rates increased over the years to more than 9% in 1970 with as much as a three-point loan fee added on. It is unlikely that you will ever be able to get a 4% mortgage again (but that's what they said in 1928).

When you buy your home through a real estate agent, the realty firm will arrange for your mortgage loan from a local financial institution, if you wish. However, check the terms. You may be able to do better if you shop around. In addition to banks and savings and loan associations, you should check insurance companies, private investors, mortgage bankers, and builders. Insurance companies are usually excellent sources for mortgage loans, but they require borrowers to buy life insurance covering the face value of the loans. Since they are really in the business of selling insurance, they may give better terms than a bank. You will have to pay extra for the insurance, but you should buy *mortgage insurance* anyway. This policy will pay off your mortgage if you die, so that your family will not be saddled with mortgage payments after you are gone.

A *conventional* mortgage is one made between the borrower and lender. You offer your home as security. The lender takes a slight risk that at any one time the value of the house will be enough to pay off the balance of the loan. As indicated above, an insurance company requires you to buy a policy covering the loan. Banks do not usually require this, although if you do buy mortgage insurance, you may be able to get better terms. With a conventional loan, there is no Government guarantee of payment.

If you are a veteran, you may be eligible for a *VA-guaranteed loan.* The Veterans Administration guarantees repayment of a large part of the loan. Because of the extra safety, lenders may give better terms for these loans than for conventional loans and may even lend money on a house with no down payment. Again, you should shop for the best terms.

FHA loans are insured by the Federal Housing Administration, but the FHA does not lend money. Because the loan is insured, lenders are more willing to accept mortgages from lower income families and to give more liberal terms. The interest rate is set by the FHA, and there is a charge of 1/2 percent for the insurance. The insurance charge is included in the monthly mortgage payments.

Farm families and families in small communities can apply for loans from the *Farmers Home Administration.* Low income families in urban areas may also qualify. Money advanced by the Farmers Home Administration may be used to buy a house, build a house, repair a home, or refinance debts on a home.

An *open-end mortgage* allows you to borrow additional funds to modernize or repair your home, without rewriting the mortgage agreement. It is desirable to have when interest rates are rising, since it enables you to borrow additional money at the original interest rate. You must be careful not to abuse this privilege, however, since it can keep you in debt for a long time. Even if you do not have an open-end mortgage, you will find that banks are usually willing to lend you money to improve your own home or to pay your bills after you have made the improvements. The fact that you own a home makes you a good credit risk. At the time of the repair loan, you will have to pay the current interest rate.

A *packaged mortgage* is a loan on the house plus any furniture and appliances included in the sale. This is undesirable because you will be paying for the equipment during the life of the mortgage, which means that your interest payments for these items will exceed the loan on them. In fact, they may be worn out and discarded before you finish paying for them.

When a lender goes to the trouble of investigating and accepting a mortgage, he would like his money to earn interest long enough to pay him for his efforts. Therefore, it is common to have a clause in the loan agreement establishing a penalty for early prepayment of the loan. Nevertheless, after a suitable waiting period of up to five years at most, you should have the privilege to pay off the mortgage in full without penalty. When interest rates drop, you will want to exercise this privilege so that you can refinance the mortgage at a lower rate.

INSURANCE

When you invest a large amount of money in a home, you want to protect the investment. You can buy insurance to reimburse you for loss caused by all sorts of calamities. There are many types of policies, and you should select those that suit your needs and pocketbook.

Fire insurance normally protects you against losses from fire and lightning. With an extended coverage clause, the policy also covers damage caused by storms, explosions, falling aircraft, riots, vehicles, and smoke.

Theft insurance covers losses from all types of theft. It may also cover "mysterious disappearance", when a valuable asset is missing, but no theft is known to have occurred. In its broad form the theft policy covers your possessions both in the home and away.

Personal liability insurance reimburses you when someone else is injured on your property and collects damages from you. If a guest trips on a rug, for example, you are liable, but the liability insurance pays the claim. It also covers damage caused by members of your family and pets.

Homeowners' insurance is a combination of all the other types of insurance. It covers all types of damage except a few specific exceptions, such as an act of war.

All insurance policies on your home are usually written with a *deductible* clause, so that the insurance company will not be bothered with nuisance claims of a few dollars. Typically, the policy may state that the company will pay only claims above $50. The higher the "deductible", the lower will be the premium on the policy.

If you incur large debts, your creditors can sue, and if they get a judgment against you, they can attach your assets. In most states, you can get a *homestead exemption* to prevent a creditor from attaching your home. In some states all homeowners have the homestead exemption automatically, while in others you must file an application with the county recorder. It is a good idea to file for this exemption before you run into debt. Note that this exemption does not protect you when your home is pledged as security for a loan, as on a mortgage.

CONDOMINIUMS

The word *condominium* means "joint ownership". In 1961, the Federal Government passed legislation to permit condominium ownership, and individual states have since passed their own statutes defining and authorizing this concept. In effect, condominium ownership means individual ownership of each unit in a multi-unit complex of apartments or buildings. A condominium complex may consist of apartments in a high-rise apartment building, garden apartments, cluster houses, or detached single-family homes. Each living unit is individually owned, but all the owners jointly own undivided shares of all the common facilities of the whole complex. Thus, all the land surrounding the buildings, all common central heating and air conditioning systems, plumbing systems, recreational facilities, hallways, lobbies, and even the roof are jointly owned by all the tenants.

Owning a condominium may be the ideal housing solution, since it combines the tax advantages of owning a house and the freedom from the responsibility associated with renting an apartment. You are responsible only for the inside of your own unit. The common facilities are managed by a board elected by an association of the owners. If a roof leaks or the outside of a dwelling unit needs painting, the management board takes care of it. Mowing the lawn, shoveling snow, and other maintenance tasks are also the responsibility of the management board. You pay a monthly fee for these management services, but if you want to go on a vacation, you can lock your door and go, knowing that everything will be cared for.

Since the individual owners usually are not experienced in running a large residential complex, it is a good idea for the owners' association to hire a professional manager. The manager should also be represented on the management board. A good professional manager can save the owners more than the expense of his salary and can do much to enhance the value of all the condominium units. He also can act as arbiter in cases where individual owners have conflicting interests.

In large cities, the condominium complex is usually a high-rise luxury apartment building. Each owner is responsible for his own apartment, but also has the use of common facilities, which may include a swimming pool, sauna bath, conference rooms, and a large hall that can be used for entertaining. Some condominium apartments have shops on the ground floor, and the rental fees pay a large part of the costs of maintaining the common facilities.

Suburban condominiums frequently offer country-club living, providing complete recreational facilities, including a golf course. The management association not only takes care of repairs and maintenance, but even plans social activities for all the individual owners.

When you buy a condominium unit, you own it just as you would a separate house. You must arrange for insurance and a mortgage on your unit, and you pay off the loan yourself. Real estate taxes are assessed on the individual units and also on the facilities held jointly. You pay your own real estate taxes, and the management association pays the taxes on the joint property. Each individual owner pays a monthly management fee to the association to cover these taxes and also other maintenance costs. The interest on your own mortgage and your own taxes may be deducted on your income tax return, but you cannot deduct any part of the monthly management fee. Nevertheless, the net cost of owning a condominium unit is usually less than that of owning an equivalent single home, and is much less than renting an equivalent apartment.

There is very little difference in the mechanics of buying a condominium unit as compared with buying a house. The title must be searched, a mortgage loan must be arranged, and a deed must be

Individual homes in a "country club" condominium complex. (*Photo courtesy of The Villages, San Jose, Cal.*)

transferred. All these are covered in the section on buying a home. The price you are charged for the unit includes your share of the common estate.

Each owner is entitled to vote on actions of the management association and this association is thus controlled by the owners. You are entitled to a percentage of votes proportional to the ratio of the value of your unit to the total value of all the units. Thus, if you own a $30,000 unit in a one-million dollar complex, you would be entitled to 3% of the total vote. In a large complex, the units may have different values, depending on size and location, and thus the owners may have different numbers of votes. The value of the common facilities is not considered in determining the owners' voting percentages.

The same sort of considerations apply when buying a condominium unit as when buying a home. Try to judge the neighborhood first. Then judge the unit. This is also covered in the section on buying

Teeing off on the golf course of a suburban condominium complex.
(*Photo courtesy of The Villages, San Jose, Cal.*)

a home. If there is a common wall between units, you should check
that the wall is soundproof and fireproof. Because you will be voting
on the actions of the owners' management association, you will interact with your neighbors more than you would if you were renting a
similar apartment. But some owners are content to abide by the decisions of the others and never get friendly with their neighbors.

If you want a large yard for your children, you may not want
to live in a condominium, although you can probably find a complex
with plenty of open space and excellent athletic facilities. However,
for most families, and especially working couples and elderly couples
whose children have grown up, the condominium concept offers unique
advantages.

A *cooperative* apartment is similar to a condominium in that
the occupants have little responsibility, but are allowed to deduct

This building houses the recreational facilities for the condominium complex, including a sewing room, billiard room, art studio, hobby shops, card rooms, and a large auditorium. A restaurant and bar in the building are for the exclusive use of residents and their guests. *(Photo courtesy of The Villages, San Jose, Cal.)*

taxes and interest on their income tax returns. There are important differences that make the cooperative less attractive. In a cooperative, the apartment building or complex is owned by a corporation. Each tenant owns a share of stock in the corporation and is entitled to one vote in its management. All expenses are shared equally, even repairs inside an individual apartment. By a special law, each tenant is allowed to deduct his share of interest and taxes on his income tax.

In a condominium, the individual owner finances his own unit and is not affected by actions of the other owners. By contrast, in a cooperative the owner corporation gets one mortgage loan for the whole apartment. The result is that the tenants are financially interdependent. If one tenant fails to make his share of the mortgage payment, the corporation must still pay the full amount. If the tenant is financially irresponsible, the other tenants will have to pay more. Also, if you make improvements in your cooperative apartment, they probably have little effect on the total value of the whole building, and thus the value of your share will not be increased. In a condominium, however, every improvement you make increases the value of your apartment.

In a condominium you can refinance your own mortgage or sell your unit without affecting your neighbors' interests. The cooperative tenant does not have this freedom. If the original mortgage on the cooperative has been reduced by more than half by payments over a period of years, any new tenant can come in only under the existing mortgage and will be required to make a larger down payment for his stock in the corporation. This may make it harder to sell your share if you want to move out of the cooperative.

MOBILE HOMES

A *mobile home* is a movable dwelling unit, completely built in a factory and transported to the homesite by a flat-bed trailer. The mobile home is not a recreational vehicle to be pulled behind your car. It is a complete home for year-round living.

A single unit mobile home may be as small as 8 feet by 29 feet and as large as 14 feet by 70 feet. The most common size has about 744 square feet of living space (12 ft × 62 ft). Two single units can be joined to make one larger home. The mobile unit as purchased at the factory, includes living room, complete kitchen, dining area, bedrooms, bathrooms, cabinets, closets, a water heater and an automatic heating system. Furniture and appliances are extra, but may also be included when the home is delivered.

If you own a lot, you can put your mobile home there and connect it to the city water supply, electric line, and sewer. However, some localities have restrictions on minimum values of a home on your lot and may prohibit you from living in a mobile home in a more expensive neighborhood. The reason for this regulation is to protect the value of the other homes in the neighborhood. Consequently, you should not buy a lot for a mobile home until you have checked to see if such restrictions exist.

When buying a mobile home, check various floor plans and pick the one that suits you. Everything but the outside walls can be moved to suit you. After you have made your choice, you have it delivered to the lot where you want to live. Unlike a conventional home, if the neighborhood deteriorates, the mobile home can be moved to a new location.

Mobile homes are much cheaper than other forms of housing, but they do not increase in value as conventional homes do with normal inflation. It is desirable to pay cash, but a mortgage can be arranged. Loans on mobile homes are at much higher interest rates and for shorter terms than for other housing, reflecting the bankers view that the value of the mobile home will not increase over a long period. Make sure you read the loan agreement carefully and understand the terms, including the interest rate, the amount of each payment and the number of payments. Loans for eligible veterans can be guaranteed by the Veterans Administration. Other loans can be insured through the Department of Housing and Urban Development. Check with the VA or HUD to determine what you must do to qualify, since these loans are much cheaper than uninsured or unguaranteed loans.

Most people who buy mobile homes settle in *mobile home parks*. These are privately owned areas. For a monthly rental, you are assigned a lot, and your home is connected to appropriate utility lines such as electricity, gas, water and sewer or septic tank. Telephone connections are extra. Mobile home parks vary in size from a few dozen homes to a few thousand. The more luxurious communities include swimming pools, sauna baths, recreation areas, meeting rooms and shops. Use of these facilities is available to all the home owners at no additional cost beyond the monthly rental for the lot.

When you settle in a mobile home park, you have no responsibility for maintaining a yard or shoveling snow. Just as in an apartment or condominium, you can lock your door and go on a vacation without worrying about maintenance. In general, you will get to know your neighbors quite well, meeting them often when using the common recreational facilities. Although the homes are close together, there is more privacy and freedom from noise than in an apartment.

If you have a mortgage on your mobile home, the interest is deductible on your income tax return. The taxes you pay are personal property taxes rather than real estate taxes but they are also deductible. The amount you pay for monthly rent is not deductible.

YOUR HOME AS AN INVESTMENT

Beginning on page 72, a cost comparison is made between owning a home and renting. In the long run, owning is shown to be cheaper, but the investment potential makes owning your own home even more attractive.

Consider again the $25,000 home mentioned in the section on cost comparison. You pay $5000 down and arrange a mortgage loan of $20,000 for 25 years at 8%. You also pay $1000 for closing costs. Your monthly payments for 25 years are:

Mortgage principal and interest	$161
Taxes, insurance, water, maintenance	$ 84
Total	$245

If you wanted to rent equivalent living quarters, your monthly rent would be about 1% of the value of the house or $250. Thus, the monthly costs for owning and renting appear to be the same. However, interest and taxes are deductible on your income tax return, so that your monthly cost when you own is decreased by the reduction in your income taxes.

At the end of the 25-year period, you can sell your home for $25,000 (assuming a stable economy). In effect, you invested $6000 out-of-pocket cost when you bought the house and you got back $25,000 at the end of the 25-year period. You pay no income tax on the $25,000 since you have no profit on the sale of the house. If you had rented during the same period, you could have put the $6000 in a savings account to draw interest. To be sure, it would grow to more than $25,000, but the interest is taxable so that your net value would probably be nearer $20,000.

A stable economy over 25 years is an impossible dream. The trend is inflationary. For the renter this means that rents increase. For the homeowner, however, mortgage payments remain constant. Although taxes, insurance, and maintenance costs increase, your net increase for the cost of shelter is less when you own than when you rent. At the end of the 25-year period, your house may be worth more than twice its value when you bought it. Now your $6000 investment has grown to $50,000. Since this represents a profit of $25,000 on the cost of the house, only $25,000 of the $50,000 is taxable, and because it is a long-term gain, it is taxable at a lower rate. There are other tax benefits when you sell your home, to be discussed later in this section.

You don't have to wait 25 years to realize the investment potential of owning. Suppose a job transfer or a desire for better housing prompts you to sell the $25,000 house at the end of three years. With average inflation, your home may have increased in value to bring you a return of $27,400 net after commissions. During the three years you have also been making payments on the mortgage principal, and this may amount to $1200. You receive $27,400 from the sale of your house and pay off the $18,800 remaining. You have left $8600, which represents a return of $2600 for three years on your original $6000 investment. In periods of rapid inflation, the return is even more dramatic.

If you sell your home at a profit and buy a better one, you also receive tax benefits. You defer all income taxes on the profit. This is not an option. You must defer income taxes, if you meet the following conditions:

1. The house you sold must have been your principal residence, and the new house must also be your principal residence.
2. You must buy the new house within a year of the sale of the old one. It can be a year earlier as well as a year later. If you sell your old home and start building a new home, you are allowed 18 months.
3. The new house must cost more than the selling price of the old one.

If you meet these conditions you pay no income tax on the profit of the sale of the old home. However, you reduce your cost basis of the new home by the amount of this profit. There is no limit to how many times you can defer the tax on the profit of such as a sale, so long as you buy a more expensive house each time.

When calculating your profit from the sale of a home, you are entitled to deduct fix-up costs, such as for painting or papering, incurred within 90 days of the sale. These are assumed to be costs of getting your home ready for sale. The costs of any permanent improvements are considered capital expenses and are added to the original cost of your home. In this category are expenses for installing a new furnace, fixing a roof, or modernizing a kitchen.

If you are over 65 years old when you sell your home, you don't have to pay income taxes on the profit associated with $20,000 of the selling price. To avail yourself of this tax benefit, you must have used the house as your principal residence for 5 of the 8 years preceding the date of sale. The 5-year period does not have to be continuous. This benefit applies even if you have deferred the taxes for profits on sales in prior years. For example, you buy a house for $20,000 and sell it for $30,000. Then you buy another house for $35,000 within a year and you defer taxes on the $10,000 profit on the old house, but your effective purchase price of the new one is $10,000 less, or $25,000. Now after age 65, you sell the second house for $50,000. Your profit is $25,000, but the profit associated with $20,000 of the sale is tax free. Since $20,000 is 2/5 of the selling price, you do not pay taxes on 2/5 of $25,000. The tax on the remaining $15,000 is at the lower capital gains rate.

Chapter Seven

Appliances

Millions of electrical appliances are sold in the United States every year. The average family buys one major appliance a year and one or more small appliances. Some of these, like an oven or a refrigerator are necessities; some, like a garbage disposer or a freezer, are conveniences but a large number of appliances are luxuries or items that are used a few times and then stored away and forgotten. The dollars spent on appliances run into the hundreds of millions, and a large part of this expenditure represents money spent unwisely or unnecessarily. It is important to learn what you should look for in buying appliances so that you will get the most for your money. It is also important to know which of the large variety of small appliances are really useful and how to spot those that are a waste of money.

The average home has too many appliances. In common use are the following:

Dishwasher	Vacuum cleaner
Clothes Washer	Toaster
Clothes Dryer	Waffle Iron
Kitchen Range	Blender
Refrigerator	Mixer
Garbage Disposer	Coffee Maker
Television set	Kitchen Fan
Electric Iron	

In addition many families have one or more of the following:

Freezer	Bun Warmer
Electric Razor	Electric Casserole
Lather Maker	Party Grill
Electric Toothbrush	Electric Skillet

A trash compactor comes under the heading of luxury appliances: you can do without them, but they are convenient. The compactor shown here reduces a week's accumulation of trash into one disposable bag. (*Photo courtesy of General Electric.*)

Hair Dryer	Table Oven
Electric Knife	Popcorn Popper
Juicer	Space Heater
Can Opener	Ice Crusher
Knife Sharpener	Electric cooking
Egg Cooker	utensils

The list is almost endless, as manufacturers continue to bring out new appliances for special purposes, such as electric bean pots, bacon cookers and face scrubbers. Before you rush out and buy any electric appliance, make sure it meets two criteria:

(1) Will the appliance enable you to do something you cannot do just as well with your present equipment?

(2) Will you use the appliance after the novelty has worn off?

If you can answer "Yes" to both questions, the appliance is probably worth buying. For example, an electric skillet works efficiently and can be set to maintain a constant temperature during cooking. However, you can cook just as easily in an ordinary skillet on a gas or electric range, controlling the temperature by controlling the burner. Further, the ordinary skillet is lighter and easier to wash than the electric. Does this mean that the electric skillet is a poor buy? Not necessarily. You don't need it for ordinary pan cooking, but if you like to prepare food at the table in the Japanese fashion, an electric skillet is probably very useful.

Some appliances do enable you to prepare food that cannot be conveniently done any other way. Examples are waffle irons, party grills, and toasters. These meet the first criterion above, but the party grill may not meet the second. Most people who buy one use it about two weeks and then put it away and forget it. If you entertain frequently and can use a party grill for hot hors d'oeuvres, it may be worth buying.

With such a large number of appliances in your home, you must certainly expect to need a large amount of repair work. If an appliance could last five years without trouble and if you had and used only twenty appliances, you would have to call a service man on the average of once every three months. A few appliances do last for five years or longer but many require service sooner. The possible repair expense and inconvenience of breakdown should be on your mind when you are thinking of buying a new appliance.

An air conditioner may be a necessity or a luxury depending on the climate where you live. This unit plugs into any 115-volt outlet and has a carrying handle so that it can be moved easily from room to room. (*Photo courtesy of Hotpoint.*)

Most large manufacturers of appliances have authorized sales and service outlets in large cities throughout the United States. These may be company-owned outlets or may be independent operators who have contracted to handle the particular lines. Some independent service operators have contracts with more than one manufacturer. In addition to the authorized dealers, large appliances are sold by department stores, discount stores, and small order houses. Small appliances are also sold by drugstores, hardware stores, and others. The important considerations in choosing a place to buy your appliance are the reputation and reliability of the dealer, the service availability if the appliance breaks down, and the price. As with any other purchase you make, your goal is to get the most for your money when you buy appliances. The dealer that advertises the lowest price is not necessarily the cheapest. You must find out what you will get for the money, and more important, what additional charges are made, such as installation and service.

Very few dealers today resort to *bait and switch* tactics or other illegal practices. However, a salesman understandably wants to make a sale and would like to sell the product that brings him the highest commission. So you can expect high pressure salesmanship when you shop for appliances. It is important to buy from reliable dealers who will stand behind the products they sell. You should also stick to the lines of well-established manufacturers. A guarantee is worthless if the manufacturer goes out of business, and the dealer who sold you the appliance refuses to acknowledge it on the grounds that it was the manufacturer's responsibility.

When you buy a small appliance, such as a toaster or electric skillet, you generally pick it out and take it home with you. Large appliances have to be delivered, and some, like dishwashers and garbage disposers need special installations. When shopping for large appliances, find out exactly what you must pay, including all delivery and installation charges. Some dealers quote a lower price, but then add installation charges, while others quote a total price including installation.

Service warranties are also variable. Is the product guaranteed for one year or five years? Exactly what is covered and how? For example, some companies guarantee to replace all defective parts *free* for a year, others charge for labor but not for the new parts. Who will do the service? Discount houses sell appliances at the lowest prices, but they do not have service personnel. They rely on the manufacturer's service organization but in general discount houses do not otherwise stand behind the products. Large department stores also rely on the manufacturer's service organization, but most large stores also feel a responsibility to their customers. If you are dissatisfied with the manufacturer's service, the large store will stand behind the products themselves, even if it means absorbing a loss to keep a customer satisfied.

Stores like Sears have their own line of products and their own service-men who are trained to repair and maintain these products.

When something goes wrong with a large appliance that is still covered by a warranty, you notify the dealer or a specified service company. Then you wait for a serviceman to call. When he arrives he may fix it on the spot, or he may have to remove it to his shop. You may find the service irritatingly slow. Unfortunately there just aren't enough competent servicemen available. You should have somewhat better results if you buy the appliance from a store that has its own service organization.

If you have an old appliance to trade in on the new one, you may be surprised to learn that the dealer is not interested in it. In fact, he may charge you extra just to remove it. If your appliance is still in running condition, you will do better to advertise it and sell it your-self. You can also donate it to a charitable organization and take a tax deduction for its fair market value.

Before you set out to buy an appliance, try to know exactly what you want. Do you want an upright or tank type vacuum cleaner? Do you want a top-loading or a front-loading clothes washer? Do you really want the party grill you saw advertised on television or will you use it for a week and then put it away and forget it? The following pages will help you decide what appliances you should have and what to look for in appliances.

AUTOMATIC WASHERS

Electrical appliances are not necessarily work savers. Quite the con-trary, a clothes washer actually makes work. Without a clothes washer, you might send your dirty clothes to a laundry with very little effort. Of course this may be expensive, and to save money you might bring your clothes to a coin-operated laundry and wash them there yourself. If this is what you do, having the washer handy in your own home would at least eliminate the drive to the self-service laundry.

From a financial standpoint, a washer does not pay for itself for several years, but as a convenience it is probably worth the money. You can wash your clothes whenever you wish. If extra overnight guests surprise you, you can wash your bed linens with little effort. For a family, the washer should be rated in the convenience class, but

The front-loading clothes washer does an excellent job and is relatively trouble-free. This model is taller than other washers so that the door is at a convenient height, eliminating the need to stoop when loading. The extra height is gained by adding a drawer for laundry aids beneath the washer. A matching dryer is on the right. (*Photo courtesy of Westinghouse.*)

an almost necessary convenience. For the single person, the washer is more of a luxury; it would never pay for itself.

There are two basic types of automatic washing machines on the market, and both wash clothes adequately if used properly. The *top-loading* machine has an agitator designed to drive the water through the clothes. This is also referred to as an *agitator-action ma-*

chine. The *front-loading tumbler action* machine has a rotating cylinder in which the clothes are tumbled about in the water. When you shop for a washer you should know the advantages of each and should buy a machine that is easy to operate, easy to repair, and economical as well as efficient.

The only real advantage of a top-loading machine is that you don't have to bend down to load it. Since a tumbler washer does not have an agitator to take up space, it will wash a larger load of clothes than a comparable sized agitator washer. Clothes must be distributed carefully in an agitator washer since an unbalanced load will stop the machine. No such care is needed in a tumbler washer. A tumbler washer uses less water and less detergent than the top loaders and washes clothes cleaner. Hence, the tumbler washer is more economical and more efficient than the top loaders. Agitator machines have lint traps that should be cleaned after each washing; tumbler machines do not need lint traps. Tumbler machines have a gentler action that causes less wear on the clothes. The drive mechanism of the tumbler machines is much simpler than that in the top loaders so that the tumbler machines last longer and are simpler and cheaper to repair. An added advantage of the front loading machine is that the top is available for storage or the machine can be installed under a kitchen counter.

As of this writing only one manufacturer offers a front loader, so it is not surprising that salesmen for other makes tend to disparage it. There is absolutely no truth to the allegation that there is danger of water pouring out the doors of a front-loader. Having to stoop to load and unload a front loading machine is really only a very minor inconvenience.

What size machine should you buy? Remember that the bigger the machine, the greater will be the initial cost and the more water and detergent it will use. Do not buy a larger machine than you need. A machine that will wash eight pounds of dry clothes is adequate for most families. You can buy larger machines with up to 18 pounds capacity, but unless your dryer is also capable of handling the extra load you will find the larger wash loads inefficient to handle.

Make sure you can operate the machine. The controls on some washers are so complicated, they would scare anyone but an engineer. You should be able to start the machine easily and to stop it in case of emergency. If it is not stopped manually it should run through all its cycles and stop automatically. If you buy a top-loader, you should be able to clean the lint trap with ease.

The matching washer and dryer shown here have extra cycles for handling permanent press and other fabrics requiring special care. *(Photo courtesy of General Electric.)*

There are many extra features added to present-day machines whose main purpose is to increase the price. You do not need automatic dispensers for detergents, bleaches, and other cleaning agents. Machines without these dispensers do an excellent cleaning job. The dispensers cost more money and are added potential service problems. Some manufacturers offer a two-speed motor in agitator washers with the thought that the slower speed will cause less wear on delicate materials. Unfortunately the slower speed also causes less cleaning action. Do not spend money for this extra unless you like long-lasting but dirty clothes.

A temperature control, on the other hand, may be desirable, especially if your laundry contains any of the new fabrics. All washers supply hot water for washing and warm water for rinsing, which is suitable for cottons and linens. Most now provide additional combinations for washing synthetics and permanent press clothes.

DRYERS

If you own a washer, you should have a dryer. A dryer is really a labor-saving device eliminating the necessity of hanging clothes up to dry and freeing the owner from the uncertainties of the weather. Clothes dried in a dryer seem cleaner than those dried in the open air.

A dryer for larger loads enables you to do your laundry less frequently. The Norge dryer shown here easily handles 20 pounds of clothes and is available using electricity or gas. *(Photo courtesy of Fedders Corporation.)*

A dryer consists simply of a rotating drum in which the clothes are tumbled while a stream of hot or warm air flows through. The air may be heated by gas or electricity. A vent is needed to carry the moisture to the outside. If you are renting you may find your landlord opposed to your cutting a hole for the vent in the wall of your house or apartment. For this reason, renters rarely own dryers.

Whether you should buy a gas or electric dryer depends on what facilities you have in the house. If you cook with electricity, you already have the necessary 220-volt line for an electric dryer. If you cook with gas, you are connected to a gas main. In either case you will need a professional installation. The gas dryer must be connected to a gas pipe. An electric dryer needs its own switch box and a good ground connection. Once installed, the dryer cannot be moved as it is attached to the vent pipe and may also be attached to a gas pipe.

Electric dryers, have a lower initial cost than gas dryers, but the operating costs are cheaper for gas, unless you live near a power dam, where electricity is cheap. When comparing prices of individual makes, be sure that the prices quoted include delivery, installation, and service contracts.

The efficiency of a dryer depends on the amount of heat that it can generate. For gas dryers, this is measured in British Thermal Units (BTU) and a minimum of 20,000 BTU should be available. The heat output of electric dryers is measured in watts, and 5,000 watts would be a barely acceptable minimum.

Like washers, dryers are offered with extra gimmicks that tend to raise the price. A good dryer needs only three temperature settings, which may be called *high, medium,* and *low.* It does not need variable speed motors or devices to sense the amount of moisture remaining. You do not need an interior light although most dryers come equipped with them. An ultraviolet lamp for sunning the clothes is an absolute waste of money. It should however, have a timing device so that you can set it to run for any preset length of time. If clothes are still damp at the end of this time, you can set it to run a little while longer. After two or three attempts you should be able to set it correctly for any given load.

A dryer should have an easily accessible lint trap that can be cleaned easily. The larger the surface area in the lint trap, the more efficient the machine is likely to be. If the lint trap is small, it fills quickly and blocks the passage of air.

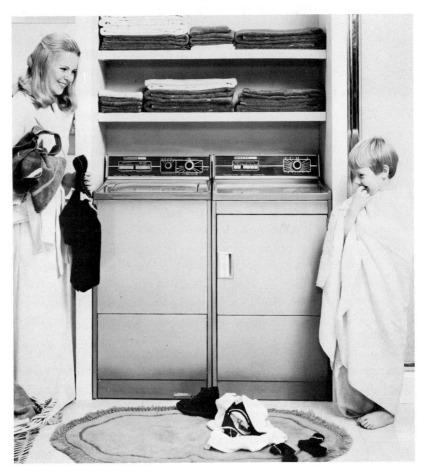

Smaller laundry machines are needed when floor space is at a premium. The Norge "Slimline" washer and dryer shown are each only 21 inches wide and handle up to 10 pounds of clothes. *(Photo courtesy of Fedders Corporation.)*

The larger the drum in the dryer, the faster the clothes will dry. However, some manufacturers offer machines that are the same size as their washers so that the two look harmonious together. Try to get a larger dryer if possible. It has a larger capacity, and for any given size load, the shorter drying time means a saving in operating costs.

Do not buy a combination washer-dryer. This is a machine that has a washer and dryer in the same cabinet. They work sequentially. It sounds like a good idea but has proved inefficient. With separate machines you can wash one load (your light clothes, for example) and then transfer that load to the dryer. While the first load is in the dryer, the washer can be at work on your second load (dark clothes). Using both machines simultaneously shortens your laundry chores. This is not possible with the combination machine.

REFRIGERATORS AND FREEZERS

A refrigerator is a necessity; a freezer is at best a convenience. Most people who own freezers do not find their food bills lower. In fact, the availability of a larger variety of foods in a freezer usually leads to fancier meals and higher food costs. If you are accustomed to entertain lavishly, a freezer may be a very convenient appliance to own, but for most families the freezer section of a modern refrigerator provides all the space needed for their frozen foods.

If you do decide to buy a freezer you must choose between an upright and a horizontal chest type model. The upright is definitely preferable. The cost of operating the chest type is slightly less than that of the upright, but not enough to be a consideration. The upright takes less floor space. Food is easily accessible in the upright, whereas, to reach something near the bottom of a fully loaded chest type freezer involves moving a large number of packages while almost doubled over the edge of the chest.

A frost-free freezer has a higher initial cost and a significantly higher operating cost than one that is defrosted manually. Since the latter needs defrosting only about once a year, it is difficult to justify the extra expense of the frost-free model. The upright freezers that require defrosting are more easily defrosted than the chest-type.

Your freezer should have an exterior warning light that glows to show that electricity is being supplied to the unit. If the light goes out, it is a sign of a power interruption which must be attended to before the food in the freezer begins to thaw.

Since a freezer usually holds several hundred dollars worth of food which can spoil in case of power failure, it is a common practice to insure the contents against this risk. An insurance policy may be included in the price of the freezer or you may have to pay extra for it. When comparing prices, find out whether insurance is included, as

The side-by-side refrigerator-freezer combination shown here has an external dispenser for ice cubes, crushed ice, or ice water. If you do a lot of entertaining or have children who constantly want a drink of water, this dispenser is worth having. (*Photo courtesy of General Electric.*)

well as delivery and installation expense. You should be aware that food does not keep indefinitely in a freezer. Some foods, such as pies, sandwiches and clams may be kept safely for only a month, and no food should be saved after a year.

If you own a freezer, you don't need a freezing compartment

The upright freezer uses more electricity than the chest models but takes up less floor space. Food is more accessible in the upright than in the chest. The model shown has 15.6 cubic feet of space and 16.9 square feet of shelf area. It needs no defrosting. (*Photo courtesy of Amana Refrigeration, Inc.*)

in your refrigerator, but try to find a refrigerator without one. Actually, there are a few models of refrigerators available without freezers, but the demand for them is so small that they cost more than the more complicated refrigerator-freezer combinations.

Many types and styles of refrigerator-freezer combinations have been manufactured in the past, but manufacturers rarely carry a complete line. Refrigerator-freezer combinations may have the freezer at top, bottom, or beside the refrigerator. Early models had one large door,

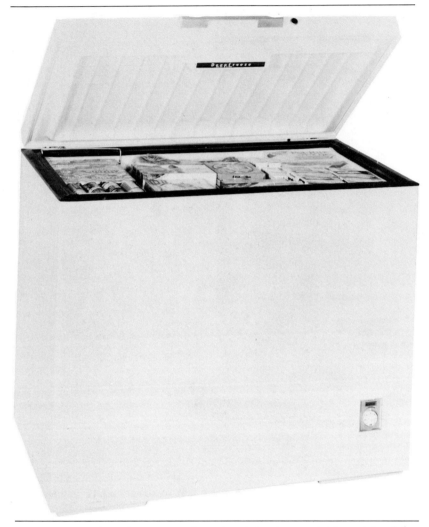

The horizontal chest freezer uses less electricity than upright models of the same capacity. Chest freezers are available in sizes ranging from seven cubic feet up. The smaller sizes can be used in the kitchen. *(Photo courtesy of Amana Refrigeration, Inc.)*

which gave access to both compartments. The freezer compartment in a one-door model is not really a freezer because it has no solid barrier separating it from the refrigerator compartment. The freezer space in these refrigerators is good for storing ice cubes, but not much else, since it does not get cold enough to protect food for any reasonable length of time. In a true refrigerator-freezer combination, the two compartments have

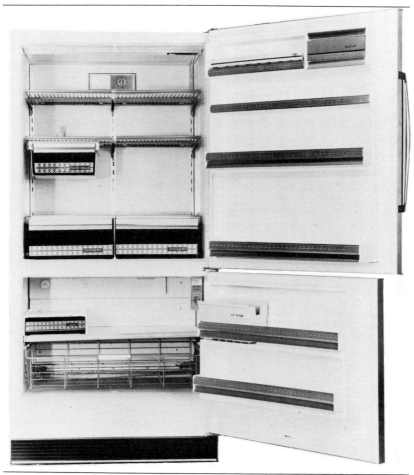

A combination refrigerator-freezer with freezer at the bottom is not as popular as other models, but is just as efficient. The model shown has separate controls for freezer and refrigerator sections and requires no defrosting. An ice maker is an optional accessory. *(Photo courtesy of Amana Refrigeration, Inc.)*

separate doors and are insulated from one another. The combination with the freezer at the top is popular and is the least expensive. Engineering problems involved with putting the freezer at the bottom have made this type more expensive than the top freezer units. Side-by-side units should be the most convenient. However, in order to hold large items of food, such as a frozen turkey, a side-by-side combination would be too large to fit in the alcoves usually allocated for refrigerators. Manufacturers do make narrow side-by-side units that are 36

Side-by-side refrigerator-freezer combinations are available in many sizes. The model shown has an 8 cu. ft. freezer and a 14 cu. ft. refrigerator, which is a convenient size for an average family. *(Photo courtesy of Amana Refrigeration, Inc.)*

inches wide or less, but they accomplish this by skimping on the thickness of the insulation and by making both the refrigerator and freezer units so narrow that the space cannot be used efficiently. If you have a lot of space for a refrigerator-freezer combination, a large side-by-side unit could be your best bet. But make sure you need that much freezer capacity. If you use a small amount of frozen foods, a top freezer unit is your best buy.

The old conventional type of refrigerator had to be defrosted about once a month. Defrosting is not difficult and takes only 15 or 20

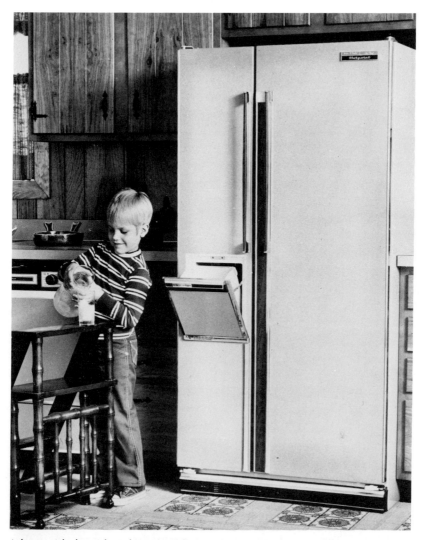

A large side-by-side refrigerator-freezer is an excellent buy for families who can use the space available. The pull-down ice cube bin on the freezer door of the model shown here is a desirable convenience when ice cubes are needed frequently. (*Photo courtesy of Hotpoint.*)

minutes when done according to the manufacturer's directions. Nevertheless, defrosting a refrigerator is one of the most disliked household chores, and American consumers are always willing to spend money to free themselves from disagreeable tasks. Manufacturers developed units that defrosted automatically and then followed with units that

The most popular type of refrigerator-freezer combination has the freezer at the top. This model has an extra-large freezer compartment. Other features included are a 7-day meat drawer and adjustable shelves in both door and interior. *(Photo courtesy of General Electric.)*

never need defrosting because no frost forms. Combinations with the freezer at the top are available in two types. In the *automatic defrost* models, the refrigerator compartment is defrosted automatically, but the freezer section must be defrosted manually about once a year. In the *no-frost* models both the freezer and the refrigerator are frost-free.

In side-by-side combinations, both sections are frost-free. It is almost impossible to buy a unit today that is defrosted manually. This is really unfortunate since frost-free units have a higher initial cost, use almost twice as much electricity, and are noisier than the old conventional units. Yet because most users want frost-free convenience, manufacturers can't sell enough conventional units to support a production line.

Most people buy refrigerators that are too small. The capacity is usually stated in cubic feet, which is a meaningless designation. More important is the usable shelf area. In terms of capacity per dollar, the unit with the freezer at the top offers the best value. How much shelf space you need depends on the size of your family and your eating habits, but if you find a large unit at a discount, you will rarely go wrong in buying it as long as it has the conveniences you need.

Your refrigerator-freezer combination should have separate controls for the two compartments. If you are about to take a short vacation, you may want to clean out the refrigerator and have it shut off while you are away, and you may want to store frozen food in the freezer during your absense.

You should have shelves in the door for eggs, butter, and small articles. The shelves in the refrigerator compartment should be removable and their positions adjustable. All interior parts should be easily removable for cleaning. Other desirable features are a vegetable crisper and a fresh meat compartment. The meat compartment is not merely a drawer for meat. It should be in a separate section, exposed to cool air (just below freezing) from a special vent. Raw meat will keep in this type of compartment for a week without spoiling.

In recent years manufacturers have been making many of the interior supports and containers in the refrigerator out of plastic instead of metal. The first plastic supports were flimsy especially in the containers and shelves in the refrigerator door. Most are now sturdy, but do look for and beware of flimsy plastic parts.

RANGES

The cooking range in the kitchen is used more frequently than any other kitchen appliance, except the refrigerator. Safety and durability are important considerations, but the person who uses the range should also be concerned with any factors that make cooking and cleaning easier. Ranges come with an assortment of gimmicks and attachments, some of which are very convenient and desirable, but all of which cost more money. Before you buy a range you should be familiar with these extras so that you can choose those that are useful.

A range should have a cooktop with four cooking units or burners and one or two ovens. It is possible to buy cook top and ovens separately and build them into the counters and cabinets in the kitchen. Separate units are more expensive than the single range, and their only advantage is one of appearance. In some locales, a range is considered part of the furniture, which the owner takes with him when he moves. Built-in ovens and cooktops are part of the house and remain for the new owners. If you rent your home, however, a range is usually included.

Your first problem is to choose between a gas and an electric range. For an electric range you will need a 220-volt line in your home; for gas, you must be connected to a gas main. Either costs money to install, but it is a one-time cost which should not affect your decision. If an electric range seems preferable, by all means add the 220-volt line. It will be useful later for other high voltage appliances and is a selling point when you want to sell your house at some future date. If your home is equipped with both services, you might also consider a combination range which has a gas cooktop and an electric oven.

Old-time gas ranges had cast iron burners in their cook tops and were virtually indestructible. Cast iron is now being replaced with cheaper materials which are not as durable. If you decide on a gas range, try to get cast iron burners even if you must pay more for them. You will save money on repairs later. Make sure any gas range you buy bears the seal of approval of the Gas Appliance Manufacturer's Association or the American Gas Association. The seal, in the form of a blue star or blue flame, indicates that the gas appliance meets specified safety standards. Gas cooktops are fully as convenient as electric cooktops, and are usually cheaper to operate in most areas.

Gas ovens do not have the flexibility and convenience of electric ovens, although the manufacturers of gas appliances would have you believe otherwise. In an electric oven you can set a timer to start the oven at some preset time and to shut off the oven at a later time so that the meal will be ready when you want it, even if you are out of the house all day. Gas ovens must be started immediately, but a timer

The traditional gas range has a separate broiler section so that it is possible to broil and bake simultaneously. The model shown is available with a self-cleaning oven. *(Photo courtesy of Caloric Corporation.)*

can be set to turn the oven down to a lower temperature when the food is cooked. The oven then keeps the food warm until you are ready to eat. If the warming cycle is on too long, the food may dry out. It is probable that manufacturers of gas ranges will soon develop reliable switches that can make a gas oven as fully automatic as an electric, but the automatic gas oven will cost more initially, although its operating costs would be less than those of an electric oven.

In a standard gas range, broiling is done in a compartment

With the broiler near the top of the oven, it is not necessary to stoop to use it. The gas range shown here has a self-cleaning oven. *(Photo courtesy of Caloric Corporation.)*

beneath the oven. This compartment is very close to the floor and to use it requires some awkward bending or stooping. To overcome this inconvenience, some manufacturers add a broiling burner at the top of the oven, at extra cost. Another solution is an extra oven with broiler, located above the cooktop, but double-oven ranges are much more expensive. If you do buy a double-oven gas range, make sure it has a broiler in the upper oven, an omission in the cheaper double-oven units.

New electric ranges can have cooktop burners that heat up just as fast as those on gas ranges. Since this is a desirable feature make sure that it is incorporated into the range you want to buy. Some manufacturers have one high wattage burner for high-speed cooking and three low wattage units for ordinary use. This should be a preferred arrangement, except that buyers tend to use the high-speed unit for everything, with the result that it burns out and must be replaced more often.

Extra gimmicks cost extra money. These are usually called options, but it is impossible to find an electric range without some of these extras. Most are not worth the extra cost. The most common extra is the automatic oven timer to turn the oven on and off at preset

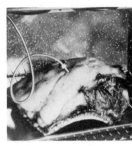

A desirable feature to look for in a range is a self-cleaning oven. It is worth the extra cost. The model shown here also has the options shown at the left: a speed broiler that broils both sides of a steak simultaneously; plug-in surface elements that can be quickly removed for cleaning or servicing; and an automatic meat thermometer to prevent overcooking a roast. *(Photo courtesy of Westinghouse.)*

times. This sounds like a good idea, but after using it for a few weeks, the novelty wears off, and you soon find you can do without it. However, it is now almost a standard "extra" and an electric oven without this gadget is very hard to find.

Other features include a deep-well burner for soups and stews, a rotisserie, a temperature sensing meat probe, and automatic temperature-controlled burners. All of these are indeed extra gimmicks that raise the cost of the range, but are not really useful. Most are ignored after their novelty has worn off.

The surface of an induction cooktop stays so cool that cooking can be done through a towel without singeing the fabric. The surface can be used as a work table even while food is cooking on it. *(Photo courtesy of Westinghouse.)*

A self-cleaning oven is the one added feature that you should buy in either a gas or electric range. Cleaning an oven is a disagreeable, time-consuming task, and the convenience of a self-cleaning oven is well worth the extra money spent for it. There are two methods of doing this. The first involves setting the oven at a temperature over 900 degrees, and this intense heat burns off the dried food on the interior surface. The second method depends on a chemical coating on the surface that cleans continuously at ordinary baking temperatures. The high-heat method is superior to the chemical coating.

Whether you buy a gas or electric range, you should think of the problem of cleaning spilled food off the burners. Burners should be easily removable. In the electric range, the burners should be plug-in units rather than wired permanently in place. Another advantage of plug-in burners is that if one fails, you can replace it yourself, saving the cost of a service call.

A microwave oven is excellent for heating a bowl of soup or a hot sandwich in a hurry, for thawing frozen foods, or for reheating leftovers. (*Photo courtesy of General Electric.*)

A ceramic cooktop has heating coils embedded in a single large sheet of a high-temperature ceramic. It is beautiful to look at and simple to clean. However, when a coil burns out, replacement is an expensive procedure.

An induction cooktop has no burners as such. Under each cooking area is an induction coil. The surface is a large ceramic sheet, but it has no heating elements embedded in it, and it doesn't get hot. When an iron or steel pan is placed above an induction coil, high-frequency currents are *induced* in the pan, and these currents produce heat. Since the surface remains cool, it can be used as a work counter while food is cooking. Any non-magnetic materials between the pan and the induction coil will not interfere with the cooking. Thus, for example, it is possible to place a towel under the pan to catch overflow drippings, and the towel will not burn.

One disadvantage of the induction cooktop is that it works only with pots and pans made of magnetic materials, such as iron or steel. It will not heat cooking utensils made of aluminum, copper, non-magnetic stainless steel, glass, or ceramic.

Safety is an important consideration in buying any gas or electric appliance. Since ranges have to meet safety standards set by their own policing organizations, there is little danger of a gas leak or an electric shock. Check whether controls are out of reach of children's hands and also check that you can operate all controls without having to reach over hot burners.

A microwave cooking oven is not a range and will not do all the things that a range can do, but what it can do is cook certain foods in a fraction of the time taken by an ordinary oven. For example, a potato can be baked in five minutes. A microwave oven is also excellent for reheating cold food or defrosting frozen food. However, there is not as much advantage as salesmen would have you believe. In a standard oven, you can bake a potato in 45 minutes, or you can bake eight potatoes in the same time. In a microwave oven, one potato does take only five minutes, but two take ten minutes and eight potatoes take almost as long as in a standard oven. For heating or cooking small quantities of food, a microwave oven is useful, and if you frequently cook for one or two, it may be a good buy.

DISHWASHERS

A dishwasher is a very popular appliance, but it is not really a necessity. People have been washing dishes by hand for years, and in general can wash dishes faster than an automatic dishwasher can. Nevertheless, washing dishes is not an enjoyable task, and any machine that eliminates an unpleasant chore is bound to be popular. On the plus side, a

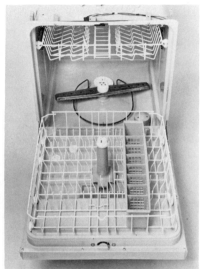

A built-in dishwasher fits under a counter and takes up no extra floor space in your kitchen. On the right is an interior view of an uninstalled dishwasher. (*Photo courtesy of Westinghouse.*)

dishwasher washes dishes cleaner than can be done manually because it is able to use hotter water than the average person can stand. Also, breakfast and lunch dishes can be stored out of sight in the dishwasher without washing. Then when the dinner dishes are added, the whole day's dishwashing can be done in one operation.

The "standard" dishwasher is a *built-in* model. It is built into the kitchen counter permanently and is connected directly to the plumbing and electricity. Built-in dishwashers load from the front and are all the same size to fit into place under the standard-size kitchen counter. This enables an architect to plan a kitchen with room for a dishwasher without having to determine what make the buyer wants. It also means that there is very little difference in capacity from one dishwasher to the next, and you should not be misled by advertising claims purporting to show that one brand of dishwasher will handle more dirty dishes than the others. However, the racks in a particular model may be designed to handle more glasses and fewer plates than the others. If you know that your dishwashing loads will include an unusually large number of glasses, this could be a consideration when you make a choice. If the built-in dishwasher is located near the center of a

A top-loading portable dishwasher rolls on casters and can be wheeled out of the way when not in use. *(Photo courtesy of Hotpoint.)*

counter, it needs only a front panel to dress it up. When the dishwasher is at the end of a counter, it also needs a side panel to dress up the side that's visible. It is also possible to have a built-in dishwasher free-standing instead of under a counter. Then it needs a top and panels on all visible sides. The more extra panels required, the more expensive the installation will be.

A *portable* dishwasher is mounted on small wheels so that it can be rolled to the sink when the dishes are to be washed. Hoses are attached to the faucets for filling and a drain hose is hooked over the kitchen sink. Since a portable unit does not have to fit into a specific space, there are many sizes and shapes available. Portables are usually top-loading, but some front-loading portables are also available. A *convertible* is a special type of front-loading portable which can be converted to a built-in.

Portables and convertibles must be grounded to prevent the danger of electric shock. This is done through a three-wire electric cord which must be plugged into a special three-hole outlet. If your kitchen does not have a three-hole outlet, you should have one installed. Do *not* try to by-pass the ground connection by using an adapter that allows you to plug a three-prong plug into a two-hole outlet. You will also have to check the electric code in your area. Some codes require that a dishwasher must be connected to a separate line that is used for nothing else.

If you are renting, you are not apt to buy a built-in dishwasher. You will prefer a portable that you can take with you whenever you move. Top-loading portables are less expensive than front-loading, but loading and removing dishes from the front is somewhat more convenient. A convertible is more expensive than a portable and is not worth the extra money. Buy an inexpensive portable instead and if at some future date you want a built-in, sell the portable and buy a built-in.

If you own your own home, you will probably want a built-in dishwasher, which takes up no floor space in your kitchen. However, if the dishwasher will be free-standing instead of under the counter, you will find a portable just as reliable at a much lower cost, since you do not have to pay for installation.

A variety of optional extras is available for all types of washing machines, and all cost money. The simplest machine whether portable or built-in will clean dishes efficiently. Despite manufacturer's claims, the optional extras do not improve the cleaning ability of the basic machine. Dishwashers may be found in any color to match your kitchen. Formerly, white machines were less expensive than colored ones, but the demand for color now exceeds the call for white built-ins, so you may be able to get the color you want at no additional charge.

Most machines are versatile in their operations so that by pushing a button or turning a knob you can cause the machine to skip por-

A convertible dishwasher is basically a front-loading portable that can be built into a counter later if desired. This model features a tilt-guard door to prevent the unit from toppling over. *(Photo courtesy of Westinghouse.)*

tions of the cleaning cycle or to prolong wash or rinse cycles. When you first buy a machine, you may make use of this flexibility, but the novelty soon wears off. Then you get in the habit of loading the dishes, starting the machine on its normal cycle, and ignoring it for the whole cleaning operation. The extra versatility is not worth paying extra money for. In some machines, lights on the front panel indicate what portion of the cleaning cycle is operating, but if you are not in the kitchen (and why should you be?), these lights are superfluous. Don't pay extra for signal lights. Don't pay extra for pushbuttons instead of a dial.

Other options include a long wash cycle for pots and pans and the ability to put dishes with pieces of food on them into the machine. Don't buy either of these. No machine will clean a pot which has food baked on. You will have to clean these by hand, no matter what the manufacturers say. Pots with soluble stains can be cleaned by any machine. Food put through your machine will eventually clog the filters or traps. The safe way to wash your dishes is to clean off all loose food, before loading.

When you shop for a dishwasher, find out what the total cost will be including the price of the machine, installation charges, and the cost of a service contract. Since a new machine is warranted by the manufacturer, a service contract should cover repairs and services beyond the warranty. Do not pay for a contract that duplicates the free service covered by the manufacturer's guarantee.

GARBAGE DISPOSERS

A garbage disposer may not be a necessity, but it is an excellent labor saver. This machine grinds up food wastes, even hard bones, and flushes the debris down the drain. Since this appliance does satisfy the two criteria (it has a unique job to do and you will use it), it is probably worth buying. The only reservations would be due to restrictions in your community on the use of disposers because of an inadequate sewage treatment plant.

There are two basic types, batch feed and continous feed. In a batch feed disposer, garbage is placed in the disposer, and a cap is placed in the opening and locked in place. Locking the cap actuates a switch which operates the machine. The cap has an opening in it large enough to allow water to flow into the disposer, but too small for hands and silverware. Water flowing into the machine softens the garbage and flushes the debris down the drain. In a continuous feed disposer, a wall switch actuates the operation. Food can be dropped in continuously since there is no cap. The water must be turned on while the machine is running.

A batch feed machine is usually larger and longer wearing

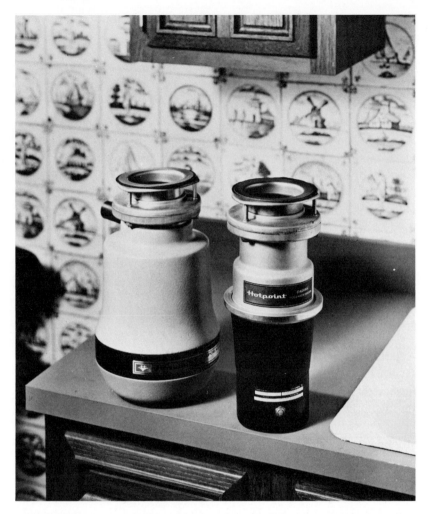

You should own a garbage disposer. Shown here are a sound-insulated model (*on the left*) and a standard unit. (*Photo courtesy of Hotpoint.*)

than a continuous feed disposer. It is also safer to use. Some new machines have reversing switches to release them when they jam, which happens to the best of them. The reversing switch is a desirable extra. When shopping for a disposer, your chief concern is to make sure the motor is powerful enough for the job. A ⅓ horsepower motor is about the smallest that can do the job adequately, and ½ horsepower is as much as you'll ever need.

You can save the installation charge on a garbage disposer by using a special kit and step-by-step instructions furnished by the manufacturer. (*Photo courtesy of Hotpoint.*)

VACUUM CLEANERS

A vacuum cleaner has only one job to do; pick up dirt. Streamlined tanks in decorator colors do not improve the cleaning ability of the vacuum cleaner, but do raise the price. There are three general types of cleaners, and you should know the advantages and disavantages of each before you buy.

The *upright* vacuum cleaner has an agitator or brush in the nozzle which beats the dirt out of the rugs so that the air flow can easily suck the dirt into the dust bag. The upright is the best cleaner for rugs. Used with attachments it can do other cleaning jobs as well.

A *canister* or *tank* type vacuum cleaner has a long hose to which various tools are attached for special cleaning jobs. This type works by suction alone and has a more powerful motor than an upright cleaner. For cleaning bare floors, draperies, furniture, and the like, this cleaner is ideal. On rugs it does an adequate job, though it lacks the beater action of an upright.

A *combination* vacuum cleaner has a canister with its high-powered motor and also a powered agitator head as one of its tools. It is excellent for every job but much more expensive than either the upright or canister cleaners. In general, it is not a good buy.

If you are a one-cleaner family, your best buy is probably a canister cleaner. However, if you have many rugs, you should have an upright with attachments. You should note that commercial cleaners, used by garages, and industries, are built for efficient cleaning and durability. These are canister machines but lack the color and styling of household vacuum cleaners. If your only concern is getting the most efficient cleaner for the money, you should buy a small commercial machine, and let someone else pay the extra price for good looks.

Before you buy any machine you should check it, preferably in your own home. Keep in mind what the machine is supposed to do, and don't be fooled by these demonstrations:

1. The machine picks up heavy objects. This is meaningless, since you rarely will want to pick up heavy objects. The question is: Will the machine suck up the dirt through a rug?

2. The machine picks up fine powder or lint. This is also meaningless, since very little suction is needed for fine powder. Your test should be made with sand or salt.

3. The new cleaner picks up dirt from a rug after your old cleaner has gone over it. No cleaner removes all the dirt with one pass. Your old cleaner would probably pick up dirt after the new machine went over the rug.

Some of the things to look for are ease of operation, dust bag capacity, noise level, and ease of emptying or replacing the bag. In an

An upright vacuum cleaner has an agitator bar or rotating brush providing a beating action with outstanding cleaning for rugs. Other features in the model shown here are a disposable bag, an indicator light showing when the bag is full, and a set of attachments for other cleaning tasks. *(Photo courtesy of the Hoover Company.)*

upright, the on-off switch should be easily accessible. The agitator should be removable so that it can be repaired or replaced when it is worn. The handle should lock in an upright position for storage. In a canister model, the tools should be made of non-corroding material such as plastic. The rug tool and bare-floor tool should swivel to permit cleaning under furniture. All tools should fasten securely to the wands, and the wands to the hose. For portability, the tank should have a carrying handle. A foot switch is preferred for starting and stopping the motor. You should also check service warranties.

Safety is an important requirement in any electrical appliance. Make sure the vacuum cleaner you intend to buy has been tested and approved by a nationally recognized laboratory. Do not accept a salesman's word that this has been done, but look for the laboratory's seal of approval. Most vacuum cleaners cannot be used on wet carpets, since moisture can cause a dangerous short circuit. If vacuuming wet carpets or outdoor carpeting is one of your requirements, look for a machine that has this capability. Such machines are available, but are not generally popular.

SMALL KITCHEN APPLIANCES

There is a large assortment of electrical appliances designed to make you spend money. A few, like an automatic toaster, are useful and desirable, but for the most part, you can cook just as well without them. Some of these make suitable gifts for brides or for the person who has everything, since they do have the appeal of novelty, but you don't really need any of them. The comments that follow aim to make you think before you buy.

Blenders and *mixers* are useful appliances if you use them. If your cooking is limited to steaks and roasts, why spend money on appliances you never use. Don't be misled by the thought that if you had a blender, you'd add more variety to your cooking. It doesn't work that way. You buy a blender, use it two or three times, and then go back to your steaks and chops. By all means buy a blender or mixer if it will make your present style of cooking easier, but don't expect it to change your style.

Electric can openers and knife sharpeners are no faster or easier to use than ordinary ones. Nor do they do a better job. Incidently, a fine steel knife should not be sharpened on anything but a good quality hone.

Electric cooking appliances have been designed for all sorts of special jobs. These appliances include waffle irons, bean pots, egg cookers, bacon cookers, roasting ovens, oven toasters, sandwich grills, casseroles, woks, fondue pots, skillets, dutch ovens, and others. New ones are constantly being invented and are advertised as suitable for wedding or Christmas presents. In general, with a few exceptions such as a waffle iron, you can cook just as well on your range using ordinary pots and pans. If you do decide to buy one of these appliances either for yourself or as a gift, the important thing to look for (which manufacturers seldom mention) is the relative ease of cleaning up after you use it. Some require extra care to keep water out of the electrical portion. Some are too heavy to move around in the sink. All are more difficult to clean than ordinary pans.

TELEVISION SETS

Modern solid state TV sets are more compact, longer lasting, and use less electricity than the old sets that had a large number of radio tubes. You can buy a color set or a black-and-white, and each comes with an assortment of options such as single-button tuning, remote control, and a variety of cabinet designs.

Size is usually specified as the length of a diagonal from upper left-hand corner to lower right-hand corner on the screen. By using the diagonal measure, manufacturers make the measurement sound bigger than it actually is. Portables with 12-inch screens are suitable when only one or two people want to watch. For comfortable viewing by a group, a 17-inch screen is a minimum. In a large room where the chairs are far from the set, you want at least a 21-inch screen.

Black-and-white sets are much cheaper than color TV's and are adequate for many programs. Black-and-white sets require less servicing and are lighter weight. There is a trend toward small, battery-operated black-and-white TV's, light enough in weight to carry with you so that you won't miss your favorite program.

If you buy a console TV, you are paying for the cabinet with no increase in viewing capability. This is a justifiable expense if you consider the TV set as a piece of furniture which should blend with the rest of the room, but you should realize that the added cost does not mean a better TV.

Most TV's have built-in antennas which are adequate for reception unless you live too far from a TV transmitter. Color sets require better antennas than do black-and-whites. You should arrange for a trial period when you buy a set, to determine if the built-in antenna is satisfactory or if you will need an outdoor antenna. An outdoor antenna is an added expense to be considered when comparing different makes. If you live far from any transmitter, you will have to rely on cable TV. For a small monthly fee, your set is connected by cable to a centrally located antenna. All programs come in clearly, and you have a choice of many channels which are not available to viewers who use their own antennas. Some set owners sign up for cable TV, even when they are able to receive local programs, because they are able to watch sports events which are blacked out locally.

Most TV sets are sold with a warranty for a specified period. When shopping, compare terms of the warranties. Who pays for parts and service? Who is responsible for getting the disabled set to the repairman? If there is a charge for a service policy, it must be added to the cost of the set. Solid state sets are quite reliable, and most reliable dealers will guarantee them without extra charge.

Safety is an important consideration in using a TV. Color sets emit X-rays which may be harmful. Learn the minimum distance for safe viewing and make sure the seating arrangement in your room will accommodate this minimum. The set should also have a seal of approval from a national laboratory, indicating it is safe to operate.

The amount of electricity used by a TV is indicated on a plate near the line cord. This is measured in watts and for simplicity may be compared to a 100-watt bulb. Thus, a 300-watt TV uses three times the electricity of a 100-watt bulb.

Single push-button or single knob tuning is a desirable feature. Without it, you may find it difficult to adjust the picture for faithful reproduction of colors. Remote control is a convenience, but not a necessity. If you think it desirable, compare the different types. Some offer only off-on and volume, others include selection of channels.

Chapter Eight

Estates

Ownership or title to property can be transferred to another by methods specified by law. In the case of personal property, title is passed by a simple sale, for cash or credit. Transfer of real property is effected by deed. While you live you can transfer title to your property to anyone. At the time of your death, title to everything you own, that is your estate, must also be passed to someone else and in general you can specify the disposition of your estate. You indicate your wishes by leaving a *will* or testament, in which case you are said to have died *testate*. If you die *intestate*, that is without a will, the law provides *rules of intestate succession*, specifying how your estate shall be divided.

Whether you leave a will or die intestate, your estate must go through *probate proceedings*. There are a few exceptions where title passes by operation of law regardless of what you say in your will. Probate proceedings are needed to determine if your will is valid and to pass the title to the rightful recipients. The proceedings also give your creditors an opportunity to be paid before your estate is distributed to others.

Probate proceedings are expensive. In addition, there are death taxes and inheritance taxes levied against your estate. If you want your heirs to receive maximum benefits from your estate, you must take steps while you are alive to put your estate in a form which will minimize taxes and probate costs. Do not think of *estate planning* as a gimmick for the very wealthy to avoid taxes. Estate planning is perfectly legitimate and can be used advantageously even by people of moderate incomes and modest estates.

COMMUNITY PROPERTY

In eight states, property acquired by a husband or wife after marriage is considered as belonging to each of them equally. The eight states are Arizona, California, Idaho, Louisiana, Nevada, New Mexico, Texas, and Washington. The important characteristic of community property is that each spouse owns half, and thus only the half owned is transferred when one spouse dies.

Community property is only certain property acquired after marriage. If a man owns a house and then marries, the house remains his *separate property*. Similarly, if a woman owns stock before marriage, the stock remains her separate property after marriage. Any income from separate property, such as rents or dividends also remains separate property. However, if the money received as income is *commingled* with community property so that it loses its identity, then this money also becomes community property. Property acquired after marriage by gift or inheritance is separate property if it was given or left to one spouse only.

In general, money that either spouse earns is community property. Thus, a man's wages are community property, and anything bought with this money, including real estate, is also community property. This means that it is possible for both separate property and community property interests to exist in the same piece of property. For example, a man makes a 25% down payment on a house. He then gets married. The 25% interest in the house is his own separate property. Then during the life of the mortgage he pays off the loan from his earnings. Since his earnings are community property, the 75% of the house that he "bought" while married is community property. His wife as her share owns half of 75% or 37½% of the house. If he wishes, he can give her a gift of 12½% of the house so that each has an equal share. In this case, the separate property interest disappears.

RULES OF INTESTATE SUCCESSION

The disposition of your estate when you die intestate is determined by a *statute of descent and distribution*. Every state has such a law, but these laws are not uniform. When real property is involved, the law of the state in which the property is located determines how that property is transferred. Thus, if a Californian dies intestate leaving real estate in California and Oregon, the two parcels may be distributed quite differently.

There are special rules that apply as between husband and wife. In most states a wife is entitled to *dower rights*. That is, she can claim a portion of her husband's estate even in cases where he left a will and stipulated that she should get less. A few states give a husband a *curtesy right*, which is a similar right in his wife's estate. Dower and curtesy rights vary from state to state. In community property states, there are no dower rights, since all property acquired after marriage is owned equally by husband and wife. In California, either spouse may dispose of the half interest he or she owns by will, but if one spouse dies intestate, the half interest automatically goes to the survivor.

In Florida a widow receives a dower right of one-third of the entire estate left by her husband, both real and personal property, whether the husband leaves a will or not. Husbands, however, have no curtesy rights. This arrangement is typical in many states, although in some states, the dower right that the wife receives is only a *life estate* in one-third of her husband's property. This means she can use it as long as she lives, but at her death it is terminated. She can, if she wishes, sell the one-third life interest during her lifetime. Typically, the property may be bequeathed to a charitable organization subject to the wife's one-third life interest. The charity may buy the interest from the widow to obtain the property free and clear without waiting for the widow to die.

In some states husbands and wives are treated equally. In Illinois, each receives a life estate in all of the decedent's real property. Other states give percentages between these two.

New York and a few other states have abolished both dower and curtesy rights. However, in these states, the surviving spouse has the option of accepting the terms of the will or of taking what would have been transferred if the decedent had died intestate. This may amount to one-half of the estate.

In all states, when a person dies intestate leaving a spouse and one or more children, the estate is shared in some specified way by the remaining spouse and the children. Usually the spouse gets between one-third and one-half of the estate, with the remainder being divided among the children. A few states have slightly different formulas for real and personal property. If there are no children and no surviving parents of the deceased, the surviving spouse usually gets the whole estate. In a few states, part of the estate goes to other living relatives of the deceased.

When a person dies intestate with no surviving spouse or child, the estate is divided among blood relatives of the deceased. In some states parents have first preference, while in others brothers and sisters prevail. The exact order is set by that state's law of descent and distribution. For example, in Pennsylvania the order is parents, brothers and sisters, grandparents, uncles and aunts. In Texas the order is parents, brothers and sisters, nieces and nephews. In Georgia, brothers and sisters get the estate.

WILLS

When you make a will, you are making a distribution of your estate, to take effect when you die. The person making a will is called the *testator* or *testatrix*. The recipients of your property are called *distributees*. The distributions themselves have special names: *devises* of real property, *bequests* of personal property, and *legacies* of money. Thus, distributees of specific property may be called devisees (for both personal and real property) or legatees (for money). Your will is a legal document, but it need not be notarized. Since you can revoke your will at any time, it is not recorded.

You must have *testamentary capacity* to make a valid will. That is, you must be sane, must know within reasonable limits what you own, and must be acting freely and without duress. If you are too young, you do not have testamentary capacity. The minimum age varies in the different states, being as low as 14 in Georgia and as high as 21 in Ohio. In most states, any member of the armed services is considered old enough to make a will, regardless of his chronological age.

Ordinarily a will must be a written document, but most states accept an *oral will* for a small amount of property. The person making an oral will must be in fear of death at the time. There must be at least two witnesses to the will, and only personal property with a value not to exceed $1000 may be bequeathed. An oral will becomes void if probate proceedings are not started within six months after the will is made.

A *holographic will* is one that is written, dated, and signed entirely in the handwriting of the testator. In theory, since the testator wrote it himself, it must be genuine, and no witnesses are required. In practice, however, the question of forgery may arise when the will is probated, if no one saw the testator write it. Holographic wills are permitted in many states for disposing of all sizes of estates.

In most cases, a will is a formal document in typewritten form, prepared by an attorney. It must be signed in the presence of two or three witnesses, the number being set by state law. It is permissible to have extra witnesses. The testator must tell the witnesses that the document is his will, but it is not necessary for the witnesses to read it. They must sign the will in the presence of the testator and of each other. Even if the laws of your state require only two witnesses to a will, it is desirable to have three. In fact, it will be necessary to have three to dispose of real property located in a state requiring three witnesses, because the laws of the state in which the property is located determine the validity of the will for this property only.

The distributees under the will should not be witnesses, although the will is not invalid if they are. Where a distributee is a witness, he is not permitted to receive more than he would if the decedent had died intestate, even if the will specifies that he get a larger amount. However, this restriction does not apply, if there are the necessary number of witnesses in addition to the distributee.

You can change your will as often as you wish. For a minor change, it isn't necessary to rewrite the whole will. You simply add a *codicil* stating the changes you desire. A codicil is an instrument adding to or altering a will slightly without revoking it. The codicil should be witnessed in the same manner as the original will.

If you move from one state to another, you may want to have a new will drawn and revoke your old one. You can cancel your old will by destroying all copies of it or by stating in your new will that all prior wills are revoked. A properly executed will is valid in all states, but may cause unnecessary complications if probated in a state far from the one in which it was made. If your will describes you as a resident of State A and then you move to State B, both states may try to levy inheritance taxes when you die. The witnesses to your will may still reside in State A. If they have to travel to State B to swear to the validity of the will during probate proceedings, your estate will have to pay for their travel expenses. The executor you named in your will in State A may not be eligible to be an executor in State B, especially if the executor is a bank incorporated and doing business only in State A. Thus, when you move to a new state, it is desirable to draw up a new will with new witnesses and a new executor. If you are not otherwise changing the terms of your will, you can simply copy it yourself and avoid legal fees. However, the legal fee for preparing a will is very moderate, and you should probably have a lawyer look over your will to make sure that no peculiarities of the law of the state to which you have moved affect the terms. For example, in some states you can disinherit children merely by failing to provide for them in your will, but in others a child omitted in your will takes an intestate share of your estate.

You can and should revise your will whenever you change your mind as to how you wish your estate to be distributed. This may occur whenever there is a change in your family status, such as a marriage, divorce, birth, or death. In states in which children can be disinherited by simply failing to mention them in a will, it is nevertheless the law that children born after the will was executed are not disinherited, on the grounds that the testator couldn't intend to disinherit them if he did not know they would exist. In most states, you must state that you want to disinherit a child or children, naming them specifically. In these states it is assumed that if you fail to mention a child, you omitted him accidentally, and then he is entitled to an intestate share of the estate. It is common practice to *cut off* a child with a legacy of one dollar. The fact that the child is remembered is thus established. In many states, a will that disinherits a child or children is examined very closely during probate proceedings for evidence of mental aberration or duress.

In most states, a marriage revokes a will as far as the benefits that are available to the surviving spouse. This means that the surviving spouse will get the same share of the estate as if the decedent died intestate. As is mentioned in the section on Rules of Intestate Succession, the surviving spouse may get the entire estate, regardless of the terms of the will. If the surviving spouse gets less, perhaps one-third to one-half of the estate, the remainder of the estate is then distributed according to the terms of the will.

Two examples will show why it is important to update your will and to seek legal counsel when you do so. In the first case, a man disinherited his daughter whom he had never seen. He had divorced his wife, the girl's mother, before the birth. His will mentioned her and cut her off with a one-dollar legacy. Subsequently, he married a woman who had no living relatives. Then the man died and his new wife received the entire estate. Unfortunately, the widow never got around to drawing up her own will and shortly thereafter she died intestate. By the rules of intestate succession in California (where she lived), since she had no living relatives, the entire estate that she inherited from her husband now descended to her husband's issue, the very daughter that the husband wanted to disinherit.

In the second case, a wealthy widow with no children executed a will leaving her estate to nephews, nieces, and favorite charities. Then she remarried. Her new husband was also financially comfortable. His new wife explained the terms of her will to him and he approved. She died first, but when her will was offered in probate, it was declared invalid as far as her surviving husband was concerned. Despite the fact that he wanted no part of his wife's estate, the entire estate went to him.

PROVISIONS IN YOUR WILL

There are no formal requirements as to the format of your will, but your intent must be clear. The will can be very short (such as "I leave everything to my wife, Mary") or can ramble on for several pages. Wills have been offered in probate that have been recorded on tape or home movies. The law states the intent must be clear, but does not state that the will must be written.

Although it is not necessary to say so, your will may begin with a statement that you are of sound mind. Presumably this is to rebut any attempts to invalidate the will on the grounds that you were mentally unbalanced. In fact, a testator is assumed to have been of sound mind unless proved otherwise.

If you have ever made any other wills and codicils, you should specifically declare them revoked in your latest will. If two different wills from the same testator are offered in probate, the court must decide which shall prevail. This can often cause long delays and expense before the estate is settled.

If you wish you can specify the details of your funeral arrangements in your will. This has no bearing on the validity of the will, and in fact is not binding on your family. However, it may save your family the need to make a decision about your funeral at a time of stress.

If you have a simple will, leaving all to your spouse, you simply so state. Usually you will include provisions for disposition of your property if your spouse predeceases you or dies as a result of the same accident.

In more complicated estates, you list all the specific bequests you wish to make. Then you may dispose of the remainder of the estate, even if you don't know how much the remainder will be. Incidentally, if you happen to refer to a bequest as a devise, the court will still allow the gift.

You may direct that all debts and costs of administration be paid. However, whether you say so or not, these expenses will be paid out of your estate before any distributions are made. Taxes are another problem. You may direct that death taxes be paid before any gifts are made. If you do not do this, the recipients will have to pay these taxes after they receive their gifts. In most cases it will make little difference, but if you have a large estate with many bequests, it would be well for you to check this matter with the lawyer who draws up your will.

At the end of the will, you name an executor to administer your estate. After you sign the will in the presence of your witnesses, the witnesses sign a clause attesting that they saw you sign it.

TITLE BY OPERATION OF LAW

When you make your will, you direct the disposition of your entire estate except for two classes of property. One class is *jointly-owned* property, and the second is *homesteads*. In both cases, title passes at the moment of your death, and the properties involved are exempt from probate proceedings.

When two or more individuals own an interest in the same piece of property, they usually have title either as *tenants in common* or as *joint tenants with right of survivorship*. Although the owners have equal shares under both types of ownership, the two are quite different legally.

When two people own a piece of property as tenants in common, they each own a one-half interest in the property. The interest is undivided. That is, it is impossible to draw a line and say "This is mine, and that's yours." Either can sell his half interest without consulting the other. If one dies, his half interest becomes part of his estate and is disposed of by the terms of his will or the rules of intestate succession.

When two people own a piece of property as joint tenants with right of survivorship, they also own undivided half interests in the property. However, if either dies, his half interest passes to the other at the moment of death *by operation of law*, regardless of any contrary provisions in the decedent's will. Every joint tenancy has this *right of survivorship* whether expressed or not.

When property is transferred to two or more people, title is taken as tenants in common, if nothing is said to the contrary. Five conditions must be met in order to create a joint tenancy. These are:

1. The parties must receive their interests at the same time.
2. The parties must receive their interests from the same legal document.
3. Each party must have the same interest.
4. Each party must have an undivided interest.
5. There must be an *expressed* intent to create a joint tenancy.

A joint tenancy is not binding forever. Either party may sell his half-interest. However, the new owner and the remaining original co-owner would now own the property as tenants in common. They could not be joint tenants since they did not meet the first two conditions above.

Tenancy by the entirety is similar to joint tenancy. The two parties must be husband and wife, and each has a right of survivorship in the other's share..Neither spouse can sell his or her half interest without the consent of the other.

The right of survivorship in joint tenancy and tenancy by the entirety causes the property to pass to the surviving party *by operation of law*. That means that probate proceedings for this property are avoided. Tenancy by the entirety applies only to real property, but joint tenancy can apply to personal property as well, including joint bank accounts and jointly owned stocks.

Many states have *homestead* laws to ensure that when a man dies, his wife and children will still have a place to live. These laws are quite varied. However, in principle they state that the homestead goes to the widow regardless of the terms of the man's will. In some states, a man can dispose of his homestead by will, but the widow can occupy it until she remarries or dies. In those states having homestead laws, the homestead passes by operation of law just as in joint tenancy. Probate proceedings are avoided. The big problem in each case is to determine exactly what is meant by a homestead. Some homes, especially mansions, do not qualify. Even lawyers differ in their interpretation of the homestead laws, and the courts may have to decide whether or not your home qualifies.

PROBATE PROCEEDINGS

Whether you leave a will or die intestate, your estate will have to be probated. Originally, the word *probate* referred to proving the validity of a will but it has come to mean the entire proceedings of executing or administering the estate of one who dies. Everything you own except for jointly owned property and homestead that pass by operation of law will be included in the probate proceedings. If you had an insurance policy on your life, the proceeds from the policy may also be included as part of your estate. However, there is a way to remove the policy proceeds from the estate, and this is discussed in the section on life insurance.

When you leave a will, the executor named in the will must file a petition for probate of the will. Usually, a lawyer draws up the petition and has the executor sign it. Then the lawyer files the petition in the appropriate court. If you die intestate, a lawyer presents to the court a petition for *letters of administration.* This petition asks the court to appoint an *administrator* to handle the estate. Frequently, the lawyer filing the petition is named administrator. Both the executor and administrator have the same duties and obligations.

Anything you can do to make the job easier for your executor will shorten the time to settle your estate. This means also that expenses will be less, and your heirs will receive more. You should be acquainted with the probate proceedings to understand the steps you can take to minimize expenses. The first step in the procedure is to establish that death has in fact occurred. Then the will, if there is one, must be proved. This is done by having one or more witnesses to the will sign an affidavit to that effect before the court.

The executor or administrator may be required to furnish a bond to make sure he doesn't abscond with the estate, since the estate is in his control until all distributions are made. Sometimes a judge may waive the requirement for a bond, when the estate is small and a relative of the deceased is named as executor. If the executor is a bank, no bond is required.

When the judge is satisfied that all legal requirements are met, he issues an order stating that the executor or administrator is qualified to handle the estate. In the case of an executor, the judge's order is called *letters testamentary;* in the case of an administrator, it is called *letters of administration.*

The executor immediately takes possession of all assets of your estate, except those that pass by operation of law. This may pose a problem for your family, especially if they were dependent on your earnings. Your will may provide an adequate income for your wife and children out of your estate, but it might take several months before the will is settled. To provide for your family if they are short of funds every state permits the executor to pay the family a *family allowance* out of the proceeds of the estate. This continues until the estate is finally distributed. The family allowance payments are considered advances against distributions that will be due when the estate is finally settled. The amount of the family allowance varies in the different states.

If you think the family allowance is insufficient to cover your family's needs, there are steps you can take before you die to make sure your family has enough money to live on. If you have life insurance, the proceeds are paid to your beneficiary immediately. This money may be part of your estate, and your executor must arrange to pay taxes for the proceeds of the policy, but the money does not have to go through the executor's hands. Another possibility is to have savings and checking accounts jointly held so that your wife gets them immediately on your death by operation of law.

Before your executor can make any distribution from your estate, he must pay off all creditors who have or had a legal claim against you. Since your executor will be unaware of your debts, he publishes a notice of your death in local newspapers and asks creditors to file their claims. In most states, creditors have up to six months to file claims, but a few states permit up to a year. The executor, then, cannot make any distributions during this waiting period. In the meantime, your executor takes an inventory of all your assets. This inventory must be filed with the court within three months of your death. Frequently it will be necessary to have assets appraised.

All claims filed by creditors must be approved by the court. As soon as they are approved, the executor pays them from the assets of the estate. If the estate has insufficient cash, the executor must sell real or personal property to raise the money. In most states, court approval is necessary to make the sale, although the executor usually makes the decision as to which assets to sell. A competent executor will liquidate only what is necessary to pay claims.

During the time that the executor holds the estate, he must manage and protect all the assets. If the assets are money, stocks, and bonds, this may be a simple job. But if the decedent owned a business, the executor must run this business until it is time to distribute it to an heir or heirs. It is important to keep this in mind when selecting an executor. In fact, as your assets change during your lifetime, you may want to change executors in your will.

There are two types of taxes on your estate. The *federal estate tax* or *death tax* is a tax on your gross estate without regard to the number of beneficiaries or how much each is to get. The *state inheritance tax* is a tax imposed on each beneficiary on the value of what is received. Your executor is responsible for your estate tax, but the individual beneficiaries are responsible for their own inheritance taxes. In addition, if your estate earns money while your executor holds it, he must file an income tax return for the estate and pay taxes on the earnings. Estate taxes may be computed for the value of the estate either at time of death or as of one year later. The option is open to the executor. Thus, if the estate is large he may wait a year to see which method gives the lower tax. Naturally, no distributions can be made before then.

The federal law excludes the first $60,000 of an estate from taxation. Therefore, if your estate is less than this amount, you know that the federal government will not take part of it in taxes. If you own more than $60,000 worth of property, you should take steps to minimize the tax bite. The actions available are covered later in this chapter.

After paying taxes and claims of creditors, your executor files a petition for distribution of your property. He presents an account of all expenses paid, including his own fees and expenses, if he wishes. Executors' fees are set by state law and depend upon the size of the estate but expenses have no limit. For small estates the executor who is a relative of the deceased usually waives fees. The court issues an order for distribution, and the executor then distributes the property. Among the expenses paid are legal fees. The lawyer who handles the probate proceedings is entitled to a fee which is also tied to the size of the estate.

ESTATE PLANNING

When you die, your property will be distributed according to the terms of your will or if you die intestate, by the rules of descent and distribution. First there are expenses which must be paid from the assets of your estate, before any distribution can be made. Probate costs, including lawyers' fees and executors' fees, and death taxes (estate taxes) are the big items of expense. Anything you can do before you die to reduce these expenses will result in larger bequests to your heirs. There are legal ways of reducing or even eliminating both probate costs and estate taxes, but you should seek the advice of an estate lawyer or the trust department of a bank, or both. The elements of estate planning are joint tenancy, gifts, trusts, and insurance. How you use these depends on the size of your estate, the sizes of individual bequests, and even on your age and the ages of your beneficiaries. You may take steps to decrease or eliminate probate costs only to find that estate taxes increase. Planning means weighing the advantages and disadvantages of each of the elements to find the scheme that best fits your estate.

The Federal estate tax takes the biggest bite out of large estates. However, the first $60,000 of your estate is tax-free. If your estate is valued at $60,000 or less, your executor does not have to file an estate-tax return. If your estate exceeds this amount, your executor has 15 months after the date of your death to file an estate-tax return and pay the tax. Table 10 shows the estate tax that must be paid for estates of various sizes.

The percentage of the estate that must be paid increases as the estate increases. At the one-million dollar level, the next increment is taxed at 37%; at the two-million-dollar level, at 45%; and above $2,560,000 at 53%. For larger estates, the rates are even higher.

If a man dies, leaving his estate to his wife, the estate is taxed. Then when the woman dies, the estate is taxed again before passing to her heirs. To reduce the inequities of this double taxation of the same estate, the government in 1948 provided for a *marital deduction*. This provision states that if one spouse dies, all the assets up to one-half of the entire estate left to the surviving spouse are free of estate taxes. Thus, if a man leaves $120,000 to his wife, $60,000 is tax-free because of the marital deduction. The remaining $60,000 is tax-free because estates up to this size are not taxed. Thus, a man can leave an estate of $120,000, and as long as at least half goes to his wife, there are no estate taxes to pay. Note that if the man left $80,000 to his wife and $40,000 to children or other relatives, there still would be no estate tax. The marital deduction of half of the estate applies as

TABLE 10 ESTATE TAXES

Gross Estate	Tax	Gross Estate	Tax
$ 60,000	0	$ 200,000	32,700
70,000	500	300,000	62,700
90,000	3,000	500,000	126,500
110,000	7,000	1,000,000	303,500
150,000	17,900		

TABLE 11   Estate Taxes Figures with Qualifying Marital Deduction

Gross Estate	$120,000	150,000	300,000	500,000	1,000,000
Tax Qualifying for 50 Percent Deduction	$ 0	1,050	17,000	47,700	126,500

long as the wife gets at least half. The remaining $60,000 could be divided in any way. If the decedent left only $50,000 to his wife and $70,000 to others, then only the $50,000 to his wife could be taken as the marital deduction. Taxes of $500, as shown in Table 10 would have to be paid on the $70,000 remaining in the estate. It follows then that when at least 50% of an estate is left to the surviving spouse, no taxes are paid on the first $120,000. Taxes on larger estates are much lower than they would be without the marital deduction. Table 11 shows representative taxes when at least 50% of the estate qualifies for the marital deduction.

A comparison of Table 10 and 11 shows the tremendous savings effected by the marital deduction.

It should be noted that the marital deduction does not apply in computing executors' fees and lawyers' fees. These fees are usually a sliding percentage of the assets that go through probate regardless of whether an estate tax is payable.

JOINT TENANCY

When you own property in joint tenancy, the other joint tenant gets your interest when you die. This happens no matter what you say in your will. The property held in joint tenancy does not go through probate proceedings. However, although joint tenancy eliminates the cost of a lawyer's fees and other expenses of probate, it does not eliminate estate taxes. In fact, in some cases joint tenancy can even result in larger estate taxes. For example, assume a man is the sole wage-earner in the family and that he buys securities and property which he places in the name of his wife and himself as joint tenants. If he dies first, as he expects to, the joint tenancy will save his wife probate fees and will not cause higher estate taxes. But if she dies first, the surviving widower will find himself charged estate taxes on what is really his own property. If he had held the property in his own name, he would pay no estate tax if his wife died first.

If an estate is less than $120,000, it is probably wise for husband and wife to own it jointly. By taking advantage of the marital deduction, no estate taxes will be charged against the estate. Also, joint tenancy eliminates the cost of probate proceedings. However. if both spouses die simultaneously, the heirs to the estate would have to pay estate taxes that might have been avoided by proper use of gifts and trusts.

For larger estates, joint tenancy has advantages in some cases, but must be used with caution. For an estate of $500,000 owned jointly by husband and wife, the estate tax, from Table 11 is $47,700. This leaves a net of $452,300 for the surviving spouse. If this spouse dies shortly thereafter, there is no marital deduction to be applied. The tax, as shown in Table 10 is more than $100,000. If the man and wife each owned $250,000 separately, when the first died, the tax would be about $10,900. This is substantially less than the $47,700 tax for the whole estate. There would be probate costs, but they would be less than the savings in estate taxes. Better still, if suitable trusts had been arranged, both probate costs and estate taxes could be decreased.

Whether joint tenancy is suitable for you, depends then on the size of your estate and whether you have a spouse as a joint tenant. A widow or widower can use joint tenancy with a child, but there is no marital deduction. For estates of $60,000 or less, parent and child joint tenancies do save probate fees, and of course there are no estate taxes.

Lawyers frequently point out that if you and your wife own all your property as joint tenants, the estate could be taxed twice, once when you die, and again when she dies. However, for a moderate sized estate, joint tenancy may be best until one spouse dies. Then the surviving spouse should seek advice about possibly setting up a trust to avoid the second taxation.

GIFTS

At one time, it was possible to avoid estate taxes by giving away most of your estate before you died. Despite the natural reluctance to part with money, enough people took advantage of this method of avoiding taxes to prompt Congress to act. As a result, there are two deterrents to giving away huge sums to avoid estate taxes.

In the first place, any gift "made in contemplation of death" is considered to be made for the purpose of tax avoidance. Such a gift is considered part of the decedent's estate and is taxed at the estate tax rate. The question to be argued in the courts is when is death contemplated. If a man is on his deathbed and tries to give away his estate, there is no question. But suppose a 70 year old gives his children a large part of his estate and then lives to be 80. Were the gifts made in contemplation of death? Congress has decreed that any gift made *more than three years before death* is *not* in contemplation of death and therefore is not subject to the estate tax or probate. The corollary is that the treasury department will argue that any gift made within three years of death is subject to the estate tax. If a healthy 40 year old gives away part of his estate and is then killed in an airplane crash within three years, the treasury department probably would not press its claim. However, if a 65 year old makes gifts and then dies of cancer two years later, the treasury department would probably win. The net effect of the law is that if you want to give away part of your property before you die, you should plan on living at least three years longer.

The second deterrent is a rather hefty gift tax on large gifts. This tax is not quite as big as the estate tax, but is a heavy enough burden to discourage the wealthy from making large gifts. However, there are *exclusions*, and many do take advantage of these to avoid estate taxes later.

You are allowed to give as much as $3000 per year to as many recipients as you wish without paying a gift tax. You don't even have to report the gift. A husband and wife can make a joint gift of $6000 without reporting it, since each is entitled to the $3000 a year exclusion. In addition to this yearly exclusion for each recipient, you have a lifetime exemption of $30,000. That is, if you give more than $3000 to any one person in any year, you must report the excess, but you pay no gift tax on the first $30,000 of the extra amounts. The $30,000 lifetime exemption applies to your total gifts over $3000 a year to each person. A husband and wife who give jointly have a $60,000 lifetime exemption.

By taking advantage of the exemptions, it is possible to formulate a gift program to reduce estate taxes. Assume a widower in his sixties has an estate of a million dollars. He has two children and five grandchildren. With the spouses of the two children, there are then nine individuals to whom he can make gifts. He sets up a plan whereby he gives each of these $3000 every year for a total of $27,000. In addition, since he is entitled to an exemption of $30,000 additional once during his lifetime, he gives his two children an extra $15,000 apiece the first year only. If he lives ten years, he would have been able to give away $300,000 tax-free. It is unlikely that the treasury department would claim that the gifts made in the last three years of his life were made in contemplation of death, since the gift program started long before that.

The executor of your estate must file a report of every gift of $5000 or more that you made at any time during your life. It also falls to the executor to try to prove that the gifts you made in the last three years of your life were not made in contemplation of death. Even if you paid gift taxes on your gifts, it is quite possible that the courts will side with the treasury department over the objections of your executor. If an estate tax must be paid on these gifts, it is *not* in addition to the gift tax. The estate is simply taxed the difference between what has been paid already and the total death tax that is due.

Large gifts to charities are usually postponed until after death. If you leave money or property to one or more charitable institutions in your will, these bequests are distributed free of tax and are subtracted from the rest of your estate before the death tax on your property is determined. However, some states set limits on the amount that can be left to charity, if there are surviving relatives of the deceased.

TESTAMENTARY TRUSTS

A *testamentary trust* is a trust created by a will. The testator states that some or all of his property shall go to a *trustee* to be used for certain specific purposes. As long as the purposes are legal and not against public policy, the trust is valid, and the trustee has a duty to follow the directions creating the trust. You can, for example, direct that the trustee invest the million dollars you leave for the trust and pay your daughter $50,000 a year from the proceeds. You can place a restriction that payments are to be made only if your daughter remains a citizen of the United States. You cannot place a restriction that payments will be made only if your daughter divorces her husband, since that would be against public policy.

In creating a testamentary trust, you generally specify how the money is to be invested, who the beneficiary is, and under what conditions the trust terminates. It is important to pick a capable trustee. You may think it wise to pick your own son or other relative as trustee, so that the trust would save the fee that would have to be paid to a bank acting as trustee. However, there are several reasons why a bank is preferable. The trust department of a bank is skilled in handling trusts. The trustee must prepare records of income and expense, file tax returns, make investments and reinvestments, and make reports to the beneficiaries of the trust. The bank does this routinely, whereas an individual who is not experienced in these matters may find it a difficult and confusing task. If the trustee is an individual, he may be unable to handle the trust because of sickness or he may die. Banks do not usually get sick or die. In the event that a trustee can no longer handle the trust, a new trustee is appointed by a court.

It is possible to have *co-trustees*. These can be two or more individuals, or an individual and a bank. Thus, you may name your wife and a bank to serve as co-trustees of a trust for your wife's benefit. The bank does all the accounting and paper work, whereas policy decisions are shared.

When you create the testamentary trust, you can specify how the money is to be invested or you can let the trustee use his best judgement. You may forbid investment in one type of stock, leaving the rest open to the judgement of the trustee; or you can be restrictive and state that the funds must be invested in a specific way, such as in government bonds. If you leave the matter of investments entirely to the trustee's judgement, he is still not entirely free since most states have limitations on how trust funds can be invested.

You can specify how much is to be paid to each beneficiary. However, keep in mind that inflation may cause hardships if the beneficiary's income remains constant. Thus, you might feel your widow can live comfortably on $800 a month and specify this amount as her allotment for the rest of her life. At some point she may need more, either because of inflation or for an unusual expenditure such as to pay for a new roof or an operation. You can have an emergency clause in the will authorizing the trustee to make extra payments in certain specific cases or at the trustee's judgement.

You can limit all payments from a trust to come from income or you can provide that all income and part of the capital be paid out regularly. When the capital is exhausted, the trust ceases.

As a general rule, you cannot set up a perpetual trust. However, you can have a trust last much longer than the life of your first beneficiary. Ordinarily, your trust terminates when the beneficiary dies, and you must specify how the remaining funds are to be distributed. However, you can continue the trust with new beneficiaries. Thus, you can set up a trust for the benefit of your wife and specify that when she dies, the trust continues for the benefit of your children as long as any of them is alive. Then the trust terminates with the assets being divided among your grandchildren.

It is possible to set up two or more testamentary trusts with the same beneficiary but with different termination requirements. There can be tax advantages. You may, for example, put half your estate in a trust specifying that all income shall be paid to your widow and that she should decide how the assets are to be distributed after her death. You put the other half of your estate in a second trust, also with all income paid to your widow, but here you specify where the assets are to go on her death, as for example, to your children. Since your widow has control of the assets of the first trust, the law considers that she owns the assets. This part of the estate is tax exempt under the marital deduction. When she dies, these assets will be taxable as part of her estate.

The assets of the second trust are part of your estate and are taxed. However, when your wife dies, since she had no control of the remaining assets, they are not part of her estate and are not taxed.

Testamentary trusts can result in reduced taxes on your estate, but don't try to create them yourself. You should seek legal advice to create such a trust, to make sure that the specific trust accomplishes what you want it to do as well as saving taxes.

There are other reasons, besides considerations of taxes and probate costs, for creating a trust. If your wife has had no experience in financial matters, she may not know how to handle a huge sum left to her when you die. You may want to create a trust so that she receives a regular weekly or monthly allowance. This also protects her from fraudulent operators who try to separate widows from their money. You may also create a trust to pay for a college education for your children. Again, you are concerned that the money might be squandered if left in a lump sum.

LIVING TRUSTS

You don't have to die to create a trust. An *inter vivos trust*, or *living trust*, is one created before death. The person making the trust is called the *settlor*. In a typical living trust, the trustee is directed to pay income to the settlor, as long as the settlor lives, and then to pay income to the settlor's widow, as long as she lives. The assets are then to be distributed to the settlor's children. The trustees can be an individual or a bank. One advantage of a living trust is that your beneficiary gets the indicated income or assets immediately on your death. The assets do not go through probate. The delay and costs of probate proceedings are avoided. However, estate taxes must still be paid.

A disadvantage of a living trust is that any debts owed by the settlor at the time of his death are not paid before the assets or income are transferred to the beneficiary. If later a creditor presents a legal claim, the beneficiary must pay it. If the estate had gone through probate proceedings instead, all creditors would have had to present their claims within a specified time or be barred, and the beneficiary then receives the assets free of all debts.

A simple form of a living trust is one in which you name yourself trustee for the benefit of another. For example, you open a bank account in your own name as trustee for your nephew. Since you are the trustee, you use the funds as you see fit, even for your own personal luxuries. When you die the funds go to your nephew immediately without probate proceeding. One advantage of this type of trust is that the beneficiary, your nephew in the example, need not know about it. Later if you change your mind, you can revoke the trust. A trust in which you name yourself trustee is not legal in some states.

If you appoint a bank as trustee, the bank charges an annual fee for its services. A few states have laws regulating trustees' fees, but competition among banks keeps the price within bounds anyway. Banks may charge a fixed percentage of income or a fixed percentage of principal. In either case, the annual fee for handling a principal of $100,000 ranges between $500 and $800. For larger principals, the overall percentage is lower. For this fee, the bank protects your assets, manages your property, collects income, and makes disbursements. In addition, the bank keeps records of all transactions, and prepares tax returns as required. If you wish to avail yourself of these services, a living trust may be a good idea. However, if you are creating the trust to avoid probate costs, you will find that after a few years the bank's fees more than offset the savings of avoiding probate.

LIFE INSURANCE

The proceeds of your life insurance policies are paid directly to your beneficiaries on your death. The money does not go through probate, and therefore there are no probate costs. However, if you have not taken the precautions to prevent it, the money is considered part of your estate and is subject to death taxes. It is an unfortunate fact that the majority of policyholders are unaware of the simple steps to take to keep the proceeds out of their estate.

Suppose that the management of a company considers its chief engineer a key employee. In fact, the engineer is so important that if he died, the company would be hard pressed finding a replacement and would suffer financial loss until a new chief engineer could be hired. To protect the company, management insures the life of the chief engineer for $100,000. The company pays the premiums on the policy. If the chief engineer dies, the company immediately receives the $100,000 proceeds of the policy. It is obvious that the $100,000 is not part of the chief engineer's estate, and thus this money is not subject to estate taxes or probate proceedings. The important criterion is that the chief engineer never *owned* the insurance policy, and therefore it was never part of his estate.

In most cases, a man buys an insurance policy, naming his wife as beneficiary. As each premium falls due, the man pays it. When he dies, his wife gets the proceeds of the policy. However, since the man bought the policy and paid the premiums, he *owned* it, and the proceeds are a taxable portion of his estate.

There is no law against anyone buying a policy on the life of another. In the case of the chief engineer, the company bought and owned the policy. Thus, if a wife buys a policy on her husband's life and pays the premium herself, she is the owner of the policy. The husband must have no control over the policy in any form. Thus, he cannot reserve the right to change beneficiaries. Now when her husband dies, the proceeds from the policy are not subject to the estate tax, because her husband never owned the policy as part of his estate.

It should be clear then that insurance proceeds can be kept out of your estate, as long as you don't pay the premiums. When a man wants to buy a new policy, he should arrange to have his wife pay the premiums. She can pay by check out of a joint checking account, but she must sign the checks. If you already own policies on your own life for which you are paying premiums, transfer ownership of the policies to your wife and let her pay the premiums from now on. Note that if you die within three years of passing ownership to your wife, the treasury department will claim that it was a gift in contemplation of death, and therefore subject to the estate tax. This claim may be rebutted by a good executor. After three years, the insurance proceeds would be exempt from estate taxes.

The main drawback in this plan is that the beneficiary is irrevocable as far as the husband is concerned. Usually the policy has contingent beneficiaries in case the wife dies first or at the same time as the husband. If the wife owns the policy, she may designate other contingent beneficiaries and change them as often as she wishes, but the husband cannot make any change. Thus, if he should divorce his wife, and remarry, he cannot name his new wife as beneficiary. In fact, his first wife can continue to pay the premiums on the policy, and she will collect when he dies.

Another problem occurs if the wife dies first. The widower can just let the policy lapse. If he wishes to have the proceeds go to his children, he and his wife should have discussed this before she died. She could possibly leave the policy to her children (or even to her husband) in her will.

Another way to avoid the estate tax on insurance proceeds is to set up an insurance trust. You create a trust to buy an insurance policy on your life. The trust must be *irrevocable* so that you have no control and no ownership in the policy. The trustee is the beneficiary and may be your bank. You transfer to the trustee sufficient cash or securities so that the income each year is large enough to pay the premium. Note that this is a gift and may be subject to the gift tax. However, if it does not exceed $30,000, you can give it tax-free claiming the lifetime exemption. In fact, it can be as much as $60,000, and your wife and you can make the gift jointly, each taking the $30,000 tax exemption.

When you die, the trustee collects the proceeds of your policy tax free. Presumably your instructions to the trustee provided that the proceeds from the policy as well as any future income of the trust should be used for the benefit of your wife and children. In effect, your wife and children receive the benefit of the policy without paying estate taxes and probate fees.

Chapter Nine

Record Keeping

It has always been necessary to keep records. But as life gets more complex, more and more records are needed. Even a small company must hire at least one full-time bookkeeper just to keep records. Whether you own your own business or are an employee, you must keep your own personal records, also.

In fact, you probably keep many records without thinking of them as such. You record your checks in the stubs of your checkbook. You keep track of sales and purchases of stocks, so that you will know whether to report a gain or loss on your tax return. If you are married, you have a marriage certificate, and this should be filed in a safe place along with copies of birth certificates, military discharge papers, and other important documents. You must also save automobile title papers, the deed to your home, and other proofs of ownership.

Although the average person does not keep enough records, it is possible to go overboard with record-keeping. If you wanted to save every receipt of purchase, every canceled check, and all papers that pass through your hands, you would need an immense storage space and excellent filing system to retrieve any paper you wanted to locate. You would probably have no time for anything else but keeping records. The basic approach to proper record-keeping is to determine what you or your heirs will have to prove and to save the records that substantiate any claims. The following list includes some of the more common reasons why you need records.

1. Proof of payment.
2. In case of loss.
3. Proof of ownership.

4. Personal data.
5. For tax returns.
6. Home costs.
7. Administration of your estate.

Proof of Payment When you buy a loaf of bread and pay cash, you don't have to save the receipt to prove that you paid for it. You know you won't receive another bill for the price of the bread. However, whenever it is remotely possible that through a human or computer error you may be billed a second time, you must save your receipts or canceled checks to prove that you have paid. You don't have to save all your receipts forever. Some you will hold only for a month.

When you buy large items on charge accounts and return some items for credit, computers are prone to make errors. You may be billed twice or may not be credited for your return. Save your canceled checks until the store sends you a statement indicating your account is correct. In general, for ordinary charge accounts, including credit card purchases, each monthly statement is an acknowledgement that earlier payments have been made. You need only save your last canceled check or receipt. If you have made no purchase on an account for more than a year and have received no bills, you can throw away the last receipt.

When you purchase a magazine subscription and pay by check save the canceled check until the subscription expires. Although it happens rarely, it does happen that a publisher stops sending you the magazine even after you have received it regularly for seven or eight months. When you notify the publisher, he may write that there is no record of your subscription. This means that somewhere the record was accidentally erased in the computer. If you send a copy of your canceled check, the subscription is quickly reinstated.

In some cases, the receipt is also a *guarantee*. If you buy a rug that is guaranteed for ten years, you may receive a receipt that acknowledges payment and also states the terms of the guarantee. You should save all such receipts until the guarantee period expires.

When you are called upon to make collections in your neighborhood for a local charity, make sure you get a receipt when you turn in the funds. It saves a lot of arguing in case the money is mislaid in a desk drawer. As a general rule, get a receipt whenever you turn cash over to someone else.

In Case of Loss Suppose a fire destroyed many of your belongings or they were removed by theft. You are insured for such casualties, so you confidently notify your insurance company. Now you may be unpleasantly surprised that the company wants to argue about your claims. You may claim for example, that a dining room set cost you $1000, but the insurance company takes the position that the average dining-room set costs only $500. Since the dining-room set is completely destroyed or missing, it is impossible for you to establish its true value, *unless you have saved the receipt for payment.* The same situation may arise when a furniture mover damages a valuable table. The purchase receipt establishes without question how much you paid for the item.

Ordinarily, an insurance company will pay original cost less depreciation. Thus, if you have paid $1000 for a dining room set and owned it 5 years, the company will deduct the value of the use you had of the set during the 5-year period. If the dining-room set has a useful life of 25 years, the company deducts one-fifth of the cost or $200 for the one-fifth of the useful life during which you have had the set. Assuming that the company and you agree on the $1000 cost and five years use, the company pays you $800. However, in cases where the insured has receipts to prove the original cost of all the items stolen or destroyed, insurance companies have usually paid close to the original costs without putting too much emphasis on depreciation. Claims adjusters for insurance companies are usually very fair-minded, but they are bombarded regularly with false or inflated claims. Any time they see written proof that the claims are honest, they lean over backward to help the insured.

If you have a loss that is not covered by insurance, you are allowed a deduction for it on your income tax return. Again, to avoid argument with the Internal Revenue Service, you should be able to verify the value by means of a receipt. In fact, you should attach a copy of your receipt or estimate of damage to your tax return so that the IRS will not call you for an audit because of this one item.

Proof of Ownership If you bought a home, you received a deed as evidence of your title or ownership. You must keep this deed as long as you own your home. In most states ownership of an auto-mobile is also proved by a certificate of ownership, and this certificate must be saved as long as you own the car. When you sell your house or car you transfer ownership to the buyer, but until you do, you must preserve these records of your ownership in a safe place. In general, a proof of ownership must be saved for anything that cannot be trans-ferred without it. In addition to a car and house, you may need proof of ownership for a trailer, boat, and some other items of personal property.

Personal Data Your birth certificate and marriage certificate are important documents that you may be required to produce at various times in your life. Although you can get copies of these from the registrar or recorder in the state where the birth or marriage oc-curred, it is inconvenient and time-consuming to apply for one every time you need it. Consequently these documents should be saved as part of your records. When you married you received a marriage certificate, but birth certificates are not supplied automatically. You should apply for birth certificates for everyone in your family so that they are immediately available when needed.

Other items of personal information that you should save in-clude naturalization papers, permits to travel in foreign countries, and records of immunization. You may also want to save some personal items that have sentimental value. All of these can be filed under *personal data.*

For Tax Returns To most people, record-keeping means sav-ing receipts to substantiate deductions taken on a tax return, and it is quite probable that this represents the largest part of keeping records. On your tax return you are permitted to itemize deductions for medi-cal expenses, contributions, taxes, interest, and casualties, as well as any miscellaneous expenses you made to help you earn more money or preserve what you have. Under miscellaneous expenses, for example, you can deduct the cost of this book, the cost of a safe-deposit box used to hold stocks that you own, the cost of financial newspapers, and union dues. If you do itemize deductions, you must be prepared to prove that you actually spent the money as you indicated.

Records to substantiate tax returns can be voluminous. Each year's records should be kept separately in a large folder or box labeled with the year of the return. They should be kept for three years after the due date of the applicable tax return, since the IRS does not ordinarily audit returns more than three years old. However, it should be noted that there is no statute of limitations on willful evasion. If the IRS can prove that you knowingly cheated on your taxes, they can bring suit at any time to recover the amount due plus penalties.

Fortunately, the IRS does give you a certain amount of leeway. Property taxes and interest on your mortgage constitute the largest part of itemized deductions for most people. If you do not own a home, you do not have these large deductions. Instead of itemizing deductions, you may find it advantageous to take the standard deduction, (15% of your adjusted gross income, with a maximum of $2000.) For example, if your adjusted gross income is $15,000 and your deductible expenses amount to $1800, don't itemize deductions, but take the $2000 standard deduction instead. In fact, if your expenses add up to $2100, you may want to take the standard deduction. True, you lose $100 of deduction, but you know you will not be audited, and thus you don't have to save any receipts to prove your deductions.

Even if you itemize deductions, you don't have to save all receipts. The instructions on filing your income tax returns include tables for permissible sales-tax and gasoline-tax deductions. If you are willing to take the specified deductions, you don't have to save receipts. However, if you know your sales taxes will be unusually large, you should save receipts to prove it, since you will almost certainly be invited to prove the deduction. Again, you may be willing to settle for the deduction permitted in the table in order to save yourself the trouble of storing all the receipts.

Note that use of a car is deductible, also. If you drive to the doctor's office or a hospital or to a pharmacy to fill a prescription, you are entitled to include the cost, at 6 cents a mile, under *medical expenses.* If you use your car to do volunteer work for a charitable organization, you can also deduct 6 cents a mile under *contributions.* Under *miscellaneous* you can deduct car expense for driving to your stockbroker's office. But do keep records of all trips.

If you take a casualty loss for a theft or fire, you should be able to prove what you paid for the item stolen or destroyed. Thus, the receipts you save "in case of loss" also serve to substantiate the value for the IRS.

If you give personal property to a charitable organization always ask for a letter acknowledging the gift. Most charities are acquainted with the IRS rules and will gladly furnish the letter, even putting a value on the property. You can then deduct this value as a contribution on your tax return.

Home Costs   For tax purposes, your home that you use as your principal residence is treated differently from a house that you own but rent to others. The latter is a business and both profit and losses attributable to this business can be entered on your income tax return. Your home, however, is not a business. If you sell it at a loss, you cannot deduct the loss on your tax return, but if you make a profit, you must pay a tax on the profit. As pointed out in Chapter 6, you can defer payment of this tax by buying a new home, but eventually this tax is due.

In computing your profit when you sell your home, you must know your true cost basis. If you pay $20,000 for a small home and then add another room for $3000, that $3000 is part of the cost. In general, the costs of any capital improvements may be added to your original costs. These include expenses for a new roof, new furnace or water heater, modernizing a kitchen, and even for large scale landscaping. You cannot include costs of routine maintenance, such as for re-papering a room, patching a leaky pipe, or replacing a defective wall switch. However, *anything* you spend on your home, in the three month period before you sell it, is considered an expense of getting the house ready for sale and may be deducted from your profit.

If you have owned your home for many years, you may find it difficult to remember all the money you put into it, unless you have records of these expenses. You need a separate file or folder for your records of home costs, and you must save those records until the IRS is satisfied. This means that you must hold them until you finally include the profit from home sales on your tax return and for three years longer, the period during which the IRS can elect to do an audit of your return.

Administration of Your Estate   When you die, the executor or administrator of your estate will have to gather all necessary documents to determine the value of your property and how to dispose of this property. Your surviving spouse should know where you kept valuable papers, what insurance policies you owned, where they are, and what bank accounts and brokerage accounts you had, individually or jointly owned. Many people who keep excellent records of their current status fail to supply enough information to simplify the problems of the surviving spouse and the executor.

An excellent tool for easing the burdens after you are gone is a small notebook listing everything that your spouse and executor must know. You should keep this booklet up-to-date, making new entries, for example, when you change your will, open or close a bank account and buy or sell property. What you enter in the notebook depends on the size of your holdings and description of valuable papers. The notebook should be kept in a prominent place among your papers, so that it will be easily found when needed. Some of the important entries are listed below.

1. The location of your will. You may also want to add the name of the attorney who you feel should handle probate.
2. Safe deposit boxes owned. Location of keys. Who may open the boxes.
3. Life insurance policies. Location. Whom to notify to claim benefits.
4. Other insurance.
5. Social security benefits. Where to apply.
6. Securities owned. Location. Name of broker(s).
7. Savings and checking accounts. Joint or individual.
8. Real property owned. Location of deeds and mortgages.
9. Location and description of anything else, your surviving spouse should know, such as title to a cemetery plot, military discharge papers, or the membership certificate for a golf club.

Chapter Ten

Theft and Fraud

Although most people are basically honest, there are too many untrustworthy individuals who are constantly trying to separate you from your money and other assets. If you are diligent about getting the most for your money it would be foolhardy then to lose any part of your property by theft or fraud. Preparedness is the best prevention.

PROTECTING YOUR HOME AGAINST THEFT

If you carry theft insurance on the personal property in your home, you are probably not worried about theft, since you believe the insurance company will pay for any loss. Unfortunately, this is not quite true. The insurance company will pay a sum equal to the initial cost of the missing property *minus depreciation*. In periods of normal inflation, the amount recovered for loss is less than the replacement cost of the stolen items. In addition, the sentimental value can never be replaced. You can rest easier if you know that you have taken all the possible steps to prevent a theft before it happens.

Any objects of unusual value in your home are a prime target for thieves especially if it is generally known that you possess them. Therefore, it is well not to seek publicity about rare paintings, expensive antiques, or jewelry. If no one knows of your valuable possessions, your home is less apt to be broken into. It may take some pleasure out of owning valuables, but you can still show them off to trusted friends.

When your home contains only the kinds of possessions owned by your neighbors there is no reason why a thief should select your home to burglarize, unless you make it easier for him by leaving doors unlocked. Conversely, if your home is more difficult to enter than those of your neighbors, the would-be thief will bypass it in favor of one that can be entered easily.

The most important protective devices are locks for your doors and windows. Ordinary spring locks are not satisfactory protection since the bolt can easily be pushed back with a knife or a piece of stiff celluloid. Make sure your locks can be opened only with a key. If your doors have double locks, most thieves will bypass your home. It is not that they couldn't pick the locks, but rather, they know that other homes can be entered more easily.

Sliding doors are especially vulnerable. There are many suitable locks for these doors, but most homes are poorly equipped in this department. Suitable locks for windows are also available. For full protection window locks should be of the type that can be opened only with a key.

Make sure that locks near glass panels can be opened only with a key. A thief can cut out a piece of a window with a glass-cutter and then reach in to open a latch that needs no key. One way to foil this method of entry is to install plastic or laminated glass in windows and door panes near locks. This type of glass cannot be cut with a glass-cutter and cannot be shattered by a heavy object.

To prevent entry through a window, you can install a grill of iron bars, so that even if the window is opened, entry is impossible. However, if the window might be a handy exit for your family in case of fire, you should have the bars equipped with hinges and a padlock so that they can be removed quickly in case of emergency.

Most burglars will not enter a home when people are present. Thus, when you and your family are away, you should try to have your home appear as if you were still occupying it. Do not pull down all the window shades. You should leave a few lights on and even a radio going. Ideally, you should put some lamps on timers so that they will go on and off at different times, as if the house were really occupied.

The best protection when you are away is a burglar alarm system. A good system protects every door and window in your home and alerts the police when an illegal entry is made. The latter is expensive, but there is an inexpensive alarm system that alerts a neighbor that can also be effective.

Do not forget the obvious. Don't leave your garage door open. Do stop deliveries of newspapers and milk. Arrange for someone to collect your mail and packages. In other words, do not make it evident that the house is empty.

PROTECTING YOUR CAR AGAINST THEFT

A thief may steal your car, or he may steal personal belongings that you left in your car. Your car insurance policy covers both types of losses, but check the policy for conditions and limitations. The amount that you can recover for loss of the car, may be limited to the original cost minus depreciation, even though the replacement cost may be much higher. For property stolen from a car, there may be a stated maximum that can be recovered. In either case, there may be a condition in the policy that *nothing* can be recovered *if the car was left unlocked.*

If you drive a late model sports car or any luxury car, you have to beware of professional thieves. They are not bothered by locks, so you have to make sure your car is never left unattended in a sparsely populated area. Park in garages rather than on a side street at night. Beware of the unattended parking lot. In general, the more lighting and pedestrian traffic there is where you leave the car, the safer it is.

If you drive an older car or an ordinary car, it will probably be ignored by professional thieves, but will still be an attraction to the youngster looking for a joy ride. Do not leave your key in the ignition, since it is an invitation to theft. Locking the car is desirable as a deterrent to the casual thief.

When personal property is left in plain view in a locked car, it is an open invitation to all kinds of thieves. A piece of luggage on the floor of a car is an attraction since it may be valuable. The thief need only break in by brute force. He doesn't have to know how to drive the car, as he would if he were planning to steal the car. You can usually leave personal property locked in the trunk of your car in reasonable safety. A thief will not risk arrest to break into a car where the possibility of finding something valuable has not been established. Of course, if you do have valuables in your trunk, don't talk about it. Note that in some of the new small cars, you can see into the trunk through the rear window. With these cars, it is not safe to leave valuables locked in the trunk.

FRAUDS

The schemes to separate you from your money are many and constantly changing. Frauds work because the victims frequently do not know that they have been cheated, and in many cases where they are aware of the fraudulent practices, they are too ashamed to admit their gullibility.

A *fraud* may be defined as any attempt to obtain money or property knowingly without giving value for what is obtained. Many fraudulent schemes may be entirely legal, and the victim has no redress. Laws may be passed later to provide penalties for these schemes, but the perpetrators then change the tactics and find new legal schemes to separate you from your money. For example, during the 1940's, a clever schemer put a classified advertisement in a Massachusetts newspaper, which read "Last chance to send in your dollar", and gave a post office box as a mailing address. Although he promised nothing, hundreds of people mailed him one-dollar bills. Some of the victims complained, but he had not done anything illegal. However, as a result of the complaints, a law was passed, prohibiting such advertisements. In effect, the law says that you must give something of value for money received. Unfortunately, the value you receive may fall far short of what you expect to get, and yet the transaction may be legal. In such a case, the victim must suffer his loss and embarrassment and has no legal remedy. Even if the scheme was an out-and-out illegal fraud, and you sue to get your money back, you may have gone to a lot of bother for nothing. In most cases of illegal fraud, you will have the satisfaction of having the culprit punished by the law, but you may find that he has insufficient funds left to repay his victims for their losses.

It is well to be on guard constantly. Be wary of something for nothing or of unusual bargains. New methods of separating a fool from his money are invented as fast as the old ones are exposed. In the sections that follow, some specific frauds are mentioned, along with warnings and steps you can take to make sure you are not among the victims.

HOME IMPROVEMENTS

Your doorbell rings, and the caller identifies himself as a painter who has just repainted a home in your neighborhood. He happened to notice that your fence needs repainting, and since he is in the neighborhood and has some paint left over, he will give you a very good price. This could be legitimate. Everything he has told you could be completely true. On the other hand, the material he may put on your fence may wash off in the first rain. Unfortunately the dishonest worker gives the whole repair industry a bad name, but there are some steps to take to separate the good from the bad.

Beware of repairmen who do not have a business address. If an address is given, make sure it exists. When a "guaranteed" job fails, you have no redress against the culprit if you can't find him. In the case of the repairman "who happened to be in the neighborhood", check with your neighbor to find out how he selected the repairman. If your neighbor tells you that he hired the man because he happened to be in the neighborhood, there is some doubt as to the repairman's honesty. There *are* honest repairmen who will sometimes check other homes in a neighborhood in which they are working. One may offer a good price to asphalt a driveway, for example, because he has some asphalt left over from the last job which would just be wasted. If he is working for a reputable firm and has a place of business where you can complain in case of trouble, you can safely take advantage of his offer. If his address cannot be checked and your neighbor does not give you satisfactory reference, it is best not to "take advantage of his offer", even though he may be honest. Better miss an opportunity, than risk the chance of loss.

On a larger scale, dishonest home improvement contractors fleece homeowners by doing legitimate repairs but charging exorbitant prices. They do this by disguising the costs. In a typical technique, the contractor may tell a debt-ridden homeowner that not only does the homeowner not have to pay cash for the improvements to his home, the contractor will even give the homeowner a few hundred dollars to pay off his debts. All the homeowner has to do is sign a second mortgage agreement. The lure of ready cash induces the homeowner to sign an agreement to make what look like small monthly payments. However, at the end of the mortgage period, usually five to seven years, the homeowner will have paid many times what the work would cost if purchased from an honest contractor. Although these deals are fraudulent and illegal, in many cases the dishonest contractors get away with them because the victims do not even realize they have been cheated.

Reliable contractors do not usually offer cash to homeowners. When you need improvements on your home, checks costs with two or more reputable contractors. If you must borrow money to finance the repairs, check with your bank or mortgagee. You will be surprised at how simple it is to borrow money for home improvements without giving a contractor an exorbitant second mortgage.

DEBT CONSOLIDATION

You have bought a car and many home appliances on the installment plan, and each month you write checks to each of your creditors. A *debt consolidator* offers to take over all your payment books for a small monthly fee. If you agree, then you write only one check to the debt consolidator and presumably he takes care of paying all your creditors.

Again, there are honest debt consolidators. However, you must be wary, since you are liable for your debts. If the debt consolidator does not pay your debts, your car or appliances may be repossessed even though you paid him to make your payments. Victims of dishonest debt consolidators have found themselves in trouble after signing agreements. Beware of all debt consolidation deals, since even the honest ones add a monthly fee to your other installment payments. A simple way to consolidate your debts is to get a personal loan from a bank or credit union. Then you can pay off all your other debts and are left with just one monthly payment to the lender.

CHAIN REFERRAL

A salesman for a color TV, a burglar alarm system for your home, an air-conditioning system, or some other expensive but popular item offers you what looks like an attractive deal. Show it to your friends, you are told, and you will get a commission of $50 (or more) on every unit that is bought through your efforts. The sad truth is that, if you fall for such a scheme, you will have to be lucky to earn even one commission, because you have paid substantially more for the item than it is worth.

Chain-referral schemes may be illegal, but they work because too often the victim is unaware he has been cheated. If you are offered such a deal, check first to see what the system or TV would cost if purchased from a reputable dealer. Make sure you include the cost of guarantees. If the prospective offer is no more expensive than a similar item purchased elsewhere, and *if the company offering it is well-established,* you probably won't lose accepting the offer, but don't count on earning commissions to help defray the cost.

FAKE CONTESTS

You receive a letter announcing that you have won a TV or a sewing machine. You merely have to select a cabinet, which you pay for. You will find that the cost of the cabinet is about what the unit in a cabinet is selling for in other stores. If you try to claim the unit without a cabinet, you may find the store reluctant to close the deal. Although you may be able to take legal steps to force them to give it to you, you will find the legal fees cost more than the item is worth. Don't bother to answer announcements that you have won a contest that you never entered.

MISSING HEIRS

When a wealthy person with a common name dies every person with the same last name becomes a potential victim for the *missing heir fraud.* Documents that appear legal are sent to thousands of families bearing the same name offering to supply information which would aid them in establishing a claim against the estate of the decedent. The cost of the information is nominal, perhaps only $10. As a result, many of the recipients send in the $10 and receive the news that the decedent left a sizable estate and information about the will. The chance that one of these sending in the $10 will share in the estate is negligible, yet the promoters of the schemes have raked in thousands of dollars.

If you are legitimately the heir of someone who dies, the executor of the estate will probably find you, since that is one of his obligations. The small fee for information may seem a small risk with a high potential return, but it is money thrown away.

UNORDERED MERCHANDISE

There are only two kinds of merchandise that can legally be sent through the mails to a person without his prior consent or agreement. The first type is free samples which must be clearly marked as such. The second is merchandise sent by a charitable organization, asking for contributions. In either case, the items sent are gifts and the recipient is under no obligation to pay. It is illegal for anyone to ship unordered merchandise and then to bill the recipient for it. In 1970, a law was enacted declaring that any wares sent through the mails and not actually ordered are unconditional gifts to the recipients.

Nevertheless, companies continue to send merchandise and then ask for payment. Many recipients pay because they feel it is too much trouble to return the merchandise. Remember, you don't have to return it. If the sender sends dunning letters, you can ignore them. If the sender remits postage and asks you to mail the goods back, you may do so, but you are not required to do so by law.

CHARITY RACKETS

If you have ever given money to a charitable cause, your name has been put on a list of those whom the charity will contact again. Because charities never have enough money, they sell these lists to anyone who will pay. The result is that you start getting mail from all sorts of charitable societies asking for donations. Many of these are worthy charities, and even the most deserving charitable societies do sell their lists. However, some societies are merely rackets to enrich the fund raisers. Some are outright frauds, and all the money contributed goes in the pockets of the fund raisers. Even some worthy charities hire professional fund raisers sometimes, and some of these fund raisers pocket as much as half the money donated.

You may feel that if you give money to a charity, it doesn't matter who gets it. You were going to give it away anyway, and you do get a tax deduction for the contribution. Perhaps you don't even want to know that the money is not being used for charitable purposes, because it would only make you feel foolish. Nevertheless, every dollar diverted to a charity racket is a dollar that a deserving charity didn't get. To ensure that your charitable donations are doing the most good, you can restrict donations to organizations with which you are familiar. If you receive an appealing letter from an unknown charity, check it with the Better Business Bureau. You should also ask for a financial statement from any unfamiliar organization, and study it to see whether most of the contributed funds are used for the stated purpose or to pay executive's salaries.

BUSINESS OPPORTUNITIES

Franchises, vending machines, distributorships, and work-at-home plans all offer the chance to get rich with little effort or investment. Most of these plans are legitimate, but countless victims spend thousands of dollars on fraudulent get-rich-quick schemes.

Beware of all schemes in which you are told that you have qualified because of your special skills or talents. How does the company know about your special talents?

If you want to buy a franchise of a well-known company, it costs money. The costs are specified in the company's standard contract, and you will be supplied with profit and loss statements of similar units so that you know what you can expect. Do not enter a franchise deal unless you can see audited financial statements of other units. Also, make sure that the company selling you the franchise will train you and make some effort to be sure the operation meets their standards.

Vending machines seem like an easy road to wealth, but operators rarely get rich. Too often an advertisement in the help-wanted section is just a bait. The ad seeks a man to service vending machines on an established route. The victim answering the ad is then given a sales pitch convincing him that he can do better owning the machines himself. He pays much more for the machines than they are worth, and then finds that the established route doesn't exist. If he is to recover anything from his machines, he must find locations for them himself.

In any prospective business opportunity, ask yourself what the chances are of recovering the amount you are asked to invest. Be realistic. How many sales are necessary to give you a good return on your investment? Will the company back you up, if special service is needed? If you have to buy any equipment and machines, are they guaranteed and by whom? Above all, make sure the company you are dealing with is well-established and reputable.

MAIL ORDER

Every year more than half a billion mail-order catalogs are sent to families throughout the country, and at least 20 million people buy something by mail. Mail-order buying offers you the conveniences of shopping without leaving your home and delivery right to your door. You can shop in any city in the country simply by answering ads in nationally published magazines and newspapers. Most reputable firms that sell by mail also offer a 30-day trial period during which you can return the purchase for any reason and get your money back. In addition to the giant mail-order houses like Sears, there are mail-order departments in most large stores and many specialty houses selling everything imaginable.

Mail-order shopping is convenient but it is also a ripe field for dishonest operators. The goods may never arrive, even though the check you mailed was cashed. Goods that do arrive may be shoddy imitations of what was pictured in the advertisements. Sometimes exorbitant charges are added for delivery, making the total cost more than what is charged locally for the same item. In some cases, goods are received damaged, and there is always the question whether they were shipped in that condition or were damaged because of poor packaging. Nevertheless, if you shop as carefully from a catalog or advertisement as you do in person, you minimize the chances of disappointment and can reap the benefits of mail-order buying.

When you buy from a reputable mail-order house or store, you don't have to worry about fraudulent practices. The mail doesn't always go through as promptly as one might wish, but these stores back up their mail-order sales just as honestly as they do their over-the-counter business. Many mail-order houses offer charge accounts to regular customers, an added convenience.

When you buy from a small specialty house, you must read the advertisement carefully. A large 6-ounce steak is no bigger than any other 6-ounce steak. As you read, skip the sales pitch and note exactly what is being offered. How long will it take for delivery? What is the delivery charge? If the ad says something indefinite such as "plus a small charge for delivery," feel free to write the company and ask exactly how small that charge is. If you never heard of the firm, check it. The Better Business Bureau is a good start. When a firm advertises in a national periodical, you can also write to the periodical to see if they have a policy of checking on advertisers before accepting ads.

Once you are satisfied that the firm is trustworthy, read the advertisement or catalog carefully for their policy on returns. Can you get your money back if you are not satisfied? Does the company reserve the right to substitute similar merchandise if they are out of what you ordered? If you are not willing to accept a substitute, make sure you specify that in your order. Allow time for delivery. During the Christmas season, deliveries are slower. If you must receive the merchandise before a certain date, make that a condition of your order.

Never send cash through the mail. All mail-order companies accept checks and money orders, and many allow you to charge on specified credit cards by simply sending them the card number. If you use a credit card, include the expiration date with your order. Make sure you include shipping charges when you pay by check or money order. If you want the item shipped C.O.D. or express collect, find out in advance what the charges will be, so you will not be in for an unpleasant surprise.

Most mail-order firms find that their biggest headaches come from illegible order blanks. Fill out the order form completely and legibly. Include catalog number, size, color, and any other descriptive information for every item ordered. Redundancy doesn't hurt, but an omission can cause a delay. Make sure to include the name and address of the person to whom the order is to be sent. If a gift card is to be enclosed, say so.

Keep a record of what you ordered. Don't throw away the catalog until the order is received. When it comes, check it as soon as possible to make sure it is what you ordered. If you are dissatisfied, let the company know immediately.

If you deal with a company that does not return your money in a reasonable time after your complaint, you have several courses of action available. One is to write to the Direct Mail Advertising Association, 230 Park Avenue, New York, NY 10017. This association will listen to your complaint, and if it appears reasonable, will help you get redress. Another course is to write to the Federal Trade Commission, Washington, D.C. 20580. The Better Business Bureau also follows up on mail-order complaints. The main thing is that you should not give in. Fraud can be rooted out only if the victims file complaints with responsible agencies that can act against the dishonest operators.

FRAUDS AGAINST THE ELDERLY

Many people over 65 are prime targets for get-rich-quick schemes, false health claims, and other plans to separate them from their money. The need for extra income, their everyday aches and pains, and their gratitude for almost any kind of attention make the elderly easy targets for illegal operators. Beware of the salesman who argues that because this is a limited offer you must sign now. Almost certainly his offer will not stand investigation. The forms and varieties of schemes to bilk the elderly are endless.

False health claims have a special appeal to the elderly person. Who doesn't have aches and pains? However, keep in mind that any amazing medical discovery will certainly be known by your physician. In fact, a major catastrophe is that some elderly people rely on the medicines they see advertised and do not see a physician until it is too late. One principal deception is a cure for arthritis, a disease that bothers millions. If there really were a cure for arthritis, doctors would be prescribing it. If you are over 65, you should have a physical examination annually, and heed your doctor rather than the advertisements.

The business-opportunities and chain-referral rackets mentioned earlier are particularly enticing to retired individuals trying to make ends meet. A frequent form is a classified advertisement in the *Help Wanted* section offering huge profits for part-time work. The person who answers the ad finds he must make an investment of some kind, maybe for inventory, before he can start reaping his profits. Needless to say, the profits never materialize.

Services that appeal to an elderly person's need for attention or companionship may be entirely legitimate. They fall in the area of fraud when they require more cash than they are worth. One example is the dance studio that entices the learner to sign a contract agreeing to pay several thousands of dollars for lessons. In all cases, investigate to find out exactly what you get for your money and seek recommendations from satisfied customers.